Roses

Easy-care roses to beautify your garden

Table of Contents

Rose Basics
page 5

Gallery of Roses
page 20

Roses in the Landscape
page 69

Index
page 92

Meredith® Books
Des Moines, Iowa

Miracle-Gro Basics – Roses
Writer: Megan McConnell Hughes
Editor: Marilyn Rogers
Contributing Designer: Studio G Design
Copy Chief: Terri Fredrickson
Publishing Operations Manager: Karen Schirm
Senior Editor, Asset and Information Manager: Phillip Morgan
Edit and Design Production Coordinator: Mary Lee Gavin
Editorial Assistant: Kathleen Stevens
Book Production Managers: Pam Kvitne, Marjorie J. Schenkelberg, Rick von Holdt, Mark Weaver
Contributing Copy Editor: Sarah Oliver Watson
Contributing Proofreaders: Terri Krueger, Stephanie Petersen
Contributing Photographers: William D. Adams: 63T, 63C, 63B; Patricia Bruno/Positive Images:
    53C; David Cavagnaro: 53B; Alan & Linda Detrick: 29T, 30T; Saxon Holt: 38CR, 46CR,
    50L, 74L, 78L; Bjanka Kadic, SPL/Photo Researchers Inc.: 41T; Rosemary Kautzky: 58TR;
    Geoff Kidd, SPL/Photo Reseachers Inc.: 26B, 29B, 41C; Marilynn McAra: 26C; Susan
    McKessar/JustOurPictures.com: 76BR; Jerry Pavia: 44, 45corner, 45, 46TR, 47corner, 62, 76L,
    78CR; Richard Shiell:13, 28, 34L, 34CR, 36L, 38TR, 40, 42CR, 48, 49corner, 50TR, 50BR,
    51corner, 56, 57corner, 59corner, 60L, 60TR, 61corner, 64TR, 66TR, 68, 70CR, 72L, 78TR;
    Sheila Terry, SPL/Photo Researchers Inc.: 41B
Contributing Photo Researcher: Susan Ferguson
Contributing Photo Stylist: Diane Witosky
Indexer: Elizabeth T. Parson
Special thanks to: Janet Anderson, Mary Irene Swartz

Meredith® Books
Executive Director, Editorial: Gregory H. Kayko
Executive Director, Design: Matt Strelecki
Managing Editor: Amy Tincher-Durik
Executive Editor/Group Manager: Benjamin W. Allen
Senior Associate Design Director: Ken Carlson
Marketing Product Manager: Isaac Petersen

Publisher and Editor in Chief: James D. Blume
Editorial Director: Linda Raglan Cunningham
Executive Director, New Business Development: Todd M. Davis
Executive Director, Sales: Ken Zagor
Director, Operations: George A. Susral
Director, Production: Douglas M. Johnston
Director, Marketing: Amy Nichols
Business Director: Jim Leonard

Vice President and General Manager: Douglas J. Guendel

Meredith Publishing Group
President: Jack Griffin
Executive Vice President: Bob Mate

Meredith Corporation
Chairman and Chief Executive Officer: William T. Kerr
President and Chief Operating Officer: Stephen M. Lacy

In Memoriam: E.T. Meredith III (1933-2003)

All of us at Meredith® Books are dedicated to providing you with information and ideas to
enhance your home and garden. We welcome your comments and suggestions. Write to us at:
Meredith Books, Garden Editorial Department, 1716 Locust St., Des Moines, IA 50309-3023.

If you would like more information on other Miracle-Gro products, call 800/225-2883 or visit us
at: www.miraclegro.com

Note to the Readers: Due to differing conditions, tools, and individual skills, Meredith Corporation
assumes no responsibility for any damages, injuries suffered, or losses incurred as a result of
following the information published in this book. Before beginning any project, review the
instructions carefully, and if any doubts or questions remain, consult local experts or authorities.

Queen of Flowers

Petal-packed flowers, sweetly intoxicating fragrance, and undeniable beauty crown roses the queen of garden flowers. They hold court magnificently among perennials, bloom happily when planted with annuals, and add a touch of floral class to shrub beds and borders.

Gardeners sometimes chide roses for their finicky ways, but hundreds of varieties bloom trouble-free for weeks on end when planted in the right growing conditions. Full sun, well-drained soil, and regular care are key to healthy roses.

Add a touch of royalty to your landscape by adorning an arbor with a climbing rose, perfuming an entryway with a fragrant shrub rose, or planting a miniature rose in a container. The wide world of roses offers a gem for almost any landscape.

< 3 >

HOW TO USE THIS BOOK

Fuss-free, no-fear roses are the focus of this book. Many featured varieties are exciting recent introductions. Some are classics that have withstood the test of time. All roses featured produce abundant flowers, have notable pest resistance, and are available through local or mail-order sources. The summary of great roses begins on page 31.

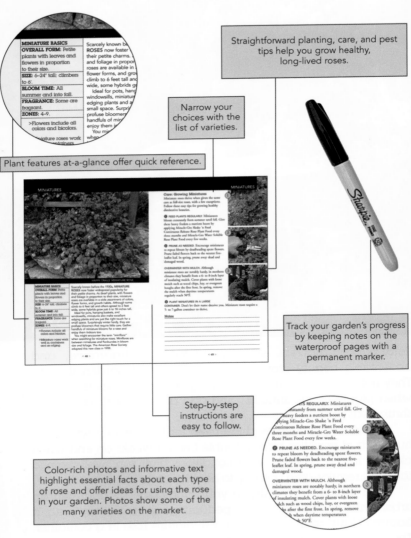

Straightforward planting, care, and pest tips help you grow healthy, long-lived roses.

Narrow your choices with the list of varieties.

Plant features at-a-glance offer quick reference.

Track your garden's progress by keeping notes on the waterproof pages with a permanent marker.

Step-by-step instructions are easy to follow.

Color-rich photos and informative text highlight essential facts about each type of rose and offer ideas for using the rose in your garden. Photos show some of the many varieties on the market.

< 4 >

When shopping for roses, it takes a heart of stone to resist the lure of a garden center's romantic blooms or the sumptuously photographed beauties in garden catalogs. In short order, your shopping basket or mail-order form can brim over with plants in need of care. Follow these basic guidelines to take the guesswork out of choosing which rose is right for you.

Consider your landscaping needs

Make rose selection easy by pairing your landscaping needs with roses that can fulfill them. For example, climbing roses effortlessly dress up fences and trellises; for cut flowers, select hybrid teas and grandifloras. Shrub roses and floribundas excel as shrub borders. Learn more about roses' landscaping roles in the "Gallery of Roses" beginning on page 31.

Know your Zone

Buy roses that are adapted to your USDA Hardiness Zone. Roses that thrive in your growing zone are most likely to survive winter unscathed and tolerate common pests in your area. Use the map on page 95 to determine your USDA Hardiness Zone. Also look for own-root roses, which require less winter protection than grafted roses.

Where to Buy

Look for roses everywhere from local garden centers to large discount stores to mail-order catalogs. ❶ Local sources often sell container, or potted, roses exclusively, but some also offer bare-root roses. While selection might be limited to a handful of varieties, container-grown roses are already established and you'll be able to see whether the top growth is healthy. They can be planted outside anytime during the growing season.

Bare-root roses are dormant plants with a few upright canes and a mass of roots. Bare-root stock is commonly offered through mail-

< 6 >

order catalogs, a resource for hundreds of varieties. Bare-root roses require immediate planting and must go in the ground in early spring to survive.

Buy a healthy plant

When buying bare-root roses, look for red or greenish canes, and make sure the root system is well-wrapped so that the delicate feeder roots haven't dried out. Container-grown plants should have healthy green leaves and two to three strong, upright canes.

Buy proven varieties

Two nonprofit groups, American Rose Society (ARS) and All-America Rose Selection (AARS), evaluate roses throughout North America. Each year, a few of the best performers receive the prestigious AARS award. Visit the groups' websites to learn more about their rating systems. Look for AARS award winners and selections with an ARS quality rating of 8 or higher on a scale of 1 to 10. These bloomers are widely adaptable to home gardens everywhere.

< 7 >

Roses will grow in a variety of conditions, but they bloom bountifully and resist insects and diseases when planted where conditions are ideal. Follow these pointers for selecting the best planting site for your roses.

PLANT IN FULL SUN. Roses need sunlight—usually at least six hours of it each day. Adequate sunlight promotes strong, healthy canes, foliage, and flower development.

A few roses will grow with less sun. 'Blue Moon', 'Christian Dior', 'Garden Party', and 'Swarthmore' hybrid teas; 'Alchymist', 'Sally Holmes', and 'Ballerina' shrub roses; 'New Dawn', a climber; and the rambler 'Etain' will grow and bloom in partial shade. However, no rose will thrive with less than four hours of bright sunshine per day.

WELL-DRAINED SOIL IS A MUST. The ideal soil for growing roses is fertile and crumbly so that it drains well, like a sandy loam.

To see how your soil compares, grab a handful of moist soil from your garden. Squeeze it into a ball. If the ball holds its shape but crumbles under a little finger-poking, the soil is loamy. If it sticks together tightly when you form it into a ball, it is clay. If it won't form a ball, your soil is on the sandy side.

The texture of soil is important because it affects the ability of roots to absorb water and oxygen. Water and nutrients quickly flow through sandy soils, so they tend to be dry and infertile. Clay soils hold water and nutrients, but they are tight soils that are difficult to work. If your soil has too much clay or too much sand, you can take steps to adjust your soil to the right texture. In general, a mix of equal parts of native soil and organic matter, such as peat moss, compost, or Miracle-Gro Garden Soil closely approximates a good loam.

Roses grow the best if they have good soil throughout their root zone. It's best to prepare the soil in the entire bed rather than individual holes. When planting just one rose, work a space at least 3 feet square. Follow these steps to amend the soil.

❶ Loosen the planting area by running a tiller over the bed or digging with a garden fork.
❷ Spread a 3-inch layer of good quality topsoil over the garden, then rototill or fork it into the native soil. Finally, spread a 2- to 4-inch layer of a mixture of two parts well-decomposed compost or Miracle-Gro Garden Soil and one part peat moss.
❸ Thoroughly mix all ingredients into the

native soil, tilling as deep as the tines will reach or up to 12 inches deep. Water well. Let the soil settle for a few days before planting.

Another soil-building solution is to use Miracle-Gro Garden Soil for Roses, enriched with Miracle-Gro plant food and other amendments. Simply dig a planting hole as described above. Backfill the hole with equal parts native soil and the Garden Soil for Roses.

GIVE ROSES PLENTY OF ROOM TO GROW. Space roses 2 to 3 feet apart. This provides good air circulation for the plants, which helps keep diseases at bay. It also gives you access to the plants so you can feed and prune as needed when the plants are fully grown.

< 9 >

Planting Roses

Good planting practices set roses on a road to a healthy, long-blooming life in the landscape. Strive to plant roses in the garden as soon as possible after purchase. Plant bare-root roses in early spring. Plant container roses from early spring to early fall.

Almost all roses have a graft union, or bud union, just between the canes and the roots. This is the spot where the rose was grafted onto the root stock. This knobby area is sensitive to cold and needs to be protected in cold climates. Plant roses so the union sits 2 inches below ground in cold-weather climates. In moderate climates, the union should be at soil level, and in warmer climates the graft union should sit slightly above the soil.

Planting a bare-root rose

❶ PRE-CARE. Hydrate bare-root roses by soaking them in a pail of water for a day before planting. For great results soak them in a vitamin B-1 solution, available at nurseries and garden centers.

PREPARE THE PLANTING HOLE. Dig a hole 2 feet wide and 2 feet deep. Amend the soil as necessary; see pages 8 and 9 for more information. Form the soil in the bottom of the hole into a cone. The cone will support roots and hold the plant in place while you fill in the rest of the hole.

❷ PRUNE ROOTS AND CANES. Prune roots back to 8 to 10 inches so they'll fit into the planting hole without crowding. Snip off damaged roots. Remove damaged canes.

❸ PLANT. Test the height of the soil cone by setting the bare-root bush on it, then laying a shovel handle across the top of the hole to make sure the graft union is at the correct level. Make adjustments as necessary by adding or removing soil. When the graft union is at the proper level, spread out the roots over the

< 10 >

cone and backfill with soil until the hole is two-thirds full.

WATER AND FINISH BACKFILLING. Slowly run water into the hole to settle the soil. ❹ After the soil has settled, finish filling in the planting hole and mound soil 8 inches over the plant to conserve water. Build up soil into a ring or make a soil dam around the plant to collect water and direct it toward the roots.

CARE. After a few weeks of careful watering and when the roots are established, buds and leaves will appear. It is now time to remove the protective mound of soil. Remove soil until the bud union is at the proper level. The bush is actively growing and adequate water continues to be important. ❺ Provide the rose with 1 to 2 inches of water per week.

Planting a container rose

Before planting a container-grown rose, be sure the soil in the container and the soil in the planting site is moist but not wet. Dig a hole about as deep as and twice as wide as the container. Amend the soil as necessary; see pages 8 and 9 for more information.

    Place the potted rose in the planting hole and make certain the graft union is at the proper level. Slit the sides of the pot with a knife and remove the rose carefully. Place it in the planting hole, then backfill around the roots halfway, pressing the soil gently around the root ball but not stamping it. Water, allow the soil to settle, and finish off with more soil. Water the rose regularly until the roots are well-established.

< 11 >

Sufficient water is crucial for healthy roses. It allows vigorous growth, optimum flowering, and strong roots. The first sign of stress from lack of water might be wilting leaves, followed by shattering flowers, shriveled flower buds, and yellowing lower leaves that eventually fall off.

Just as lack of water is detrimental to roses, too much water also has adverse effects. Too much water robs the soil and plant roots of life-giving oxygen, which is evident in symptoms similar to those of underwatering.

Large rose bushes require 2 to 5 gallons of water three times a week. In hot climates during the summer months, roses may need 3 to 5 gallons of water a day. Water as needed based on the feel of the soil an inch or so under the surface. When it feels cool and damp to the touch, but doesn't moisten your finger, it's time to water. If it feels dry, you've waited too long, and if it wets or muddies your finger, it's too soon to water.

Each time you water, wet the soil about a foot deep. For average soils, this is about an inch of water. Clay soils might need 2 inches, because water moves slowly into the soil and not as deep. Sandy soils might take only half an inch, because water readily moves through them. To ensure roses growing in sandy soil have plenty of moisture, you will need to water them several times a week.

The best way to water roses is with a drip irrigation system, ❶ a soaker hose, or ❷ a flood bubbler. These efficient systems slowly release water to the plant without runoff. They deliver water directly to the root system, keeping foliage dry, which helps avoid diseases. Control your soaker hose with a timer for easy watering. If you have only a few roses, use a watering wand or watering can to deliver water directly to the base of the plant without wetting the foliage.

< 12 >

Mulch matters

3 Help retain soil moisture and suppress weed growth with a 1- to 3-inch layer of mulch. Spread an organic mulch, such as compost, rotted manure, chopped leaves, cocoa-bean hulls, chopped bark, or Scotts Nature Scapes Color-Enhanced Mulch. Organic mulch is beneficial because it breaks down gradually and adds nutrients to the soil.

Spread mulch in spring before hot weather arrives. Maintain a 6-inch-diameter mulch-free ring around the base of plants to prevent stem rot and other diseases. Replace mulch seasonally as necessary.

Water Smart

- Water roses in early morning to reduce evaporation and allow foliage adequate time to dry.

- Deliver water directly to the base of a rose bush with a soaker hose or drip irrigation system. Avoid watering from overhead with a sprinkler or handheld hose and watering wand.

- Plan to water roses two to three times a week during dry periods, soaking the soil to a depth of 12 inches.

< 13 >

Feeding

Most roses need regular applications of plant food to reach full size and produce abundant flowers. A healthy, well-fed plant is better able to resist attacks of pests and diseases and to survive severe winter cold. Rose feeding requires an investment of only a few dollars in products and a few minutes of time for an impressive return of healthy bushes and intoxicating flowers.

When to feed

All roses benefit from an application of plant food in spring as the leaf buds begin to open. An early-season feeding provides plants with the nutrients they need to rapidly develop leaves and flowers. Repeat-blooming roses thrive with a second feeding after the first flush of flowers fades. Subsequent feeding varies by type of rose. In general, modern roses require more plant food than older cultivars.

In Zone 6 and colder, stop feeding plants eight weeks before the average date of the first fall frost to let plants harden off for their winter rest. See the "Gallery of Roses" beginning on page 31 for feeding information for specific types of roses.

What to feed

❶ The simplest way to feed roses is to use Miracle-Gro Shake 'n Feed Continuous Release Rose Plant Food or Scotts Rose & Bloom Continuous Release Plant Food. Simply scatter the granules around the base of the plant. Scratch them into the top couple inches of soil and water thoroughly. Repeat the process every two to three months as directed.

Plants absorb liquid plant food more quickly than they do granular plant foods. Mix Miracle-Gro Water Soluble Rose Plant Food with water and apply it as a supplement to longer-lasting granular plant food.

< 14 >

2

Whatever kind of plant food you use, be sure to follow exactly the directions and dosages listed on the label. Too much food or improper application can damage plants.

How to feed

For best results scratch granular plant food into the top inch or two of soil. Water plants thoroughly to carry the nutrients to the roots.

❷ When applying liquid plant food, use a hose-end sprayer made specifically for this purpose. These handy gadgets allow you to dispense a measured amount of water-soluble food as you water.

< 15 >

Pruning

Essential to good growth and flowering, pruning is part of caring for a rose, like watering and feeding. Pruning roses intimidates some new gardeners, but it is simple with our straightforward tips and techniques. There are three main reasons to prune.

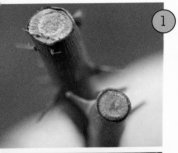

① FOR HEALTH. Dead or damaged canes should be cut back to green wood in late winter or early spring, before the plant resumes growth. ❶ Dead canes are brown and brittle. Live canes are green and bendable. Remove diseased canes when you notice them. Also remove canes growing into the center of the plant to improve air.

② FOR APPEARANCE. Bushy modern roses need help to maintain their compact, open form. Heirloom roses require less pruning because their lax, twiggy look is part of their charm. Deadheading, or cutting off spent flowers, encourages plants to rebloom and helps the plants look neat and clean.

FOR CONTROL. Some roses grow with wild abandon. Keep them within bounds by pruning their tips or entire canes anytime.

③ Pruning techniques

Generally, prune roses according to the climate and the calendar; the ideal time to start is when growth buds swell in the spring. However, pruning rules vary somewhat with the type of rose. Learn about the specific pruning techniques in the "Gallery of Roses" beginning on page 31.

Pruning can be a scratchy job, so wear gloves and a long-sleeve shirt or jacket to protect your skin against thorns.

The first step in pruning any rose is to remove dead, damaged, diseased, or weak and

< 16 >

thin canes, cutting them off flush with the bud union. ❷ Next, remove canes that are growing into the center of the plant, or those that cross each other. Canes that grow inward keep light and air from the center of the plant and will eventually cross, chafing one another. These abrasions can become entry points for insects and diseases. Using shears, cut these canes down to their origin. Strive to keep the center of the plant open to let in sunshine and allow air to circulate freely.

When pruning interior and crossing canes, aim to create a vase-shape bush with an open center. ❸ Cut canes at a 45-degree angle just above an outward-facing leaf bud (swelling on the cane). Keep pruners sharp to make clean cuts.

< 17 >

In early spring, about the time forsythia and daffodils bloom, roses begin to wake up from their long winter's nap. This is a good time to plant or prune roses—and an important time to feed them. It is also a good time to move an established rose.

PLANT BARE-ROOT ROSES. Plant bare-root roses in early spring so they can establish roots while temperatures are cool. If you wait until late spring or summer to plant roses, buy potted plants. For step-by-step planting directions, see page 10.

REMOVE WINTER PROTECTION. If you use winter covering, remove it gradually when temperatures warm. Be very careful not to break any new canes that may have emerged.

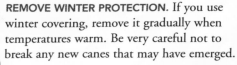

PRUNE. Cut dead or damaged canes back to green wood in late winter or early spring, before the plant resumes growth. For more pruning tips and techniques, see page 16.

FEED PLANTS. Spring is one of the most important times to feed roses. Because they are actively growing during this season, they need the extra nutrients to expand their stems and leaves. Spread rose food around established and newly planted roses beginning in early spring and repeat throughout the growing season. For step-by-step directions, see page 14

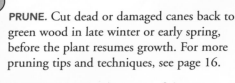

TRAIN CLIMBERS. Start to train your climber as soon as it's planted. Gently bend young, actively growing canes in the direction you want. Tie down the tips with twine, rose clips (available at garden centers), or nylon cord. Avoid tight ties that won't allow canes to expand as they grow.

< 18 >

TRANSPLANT ESTABLISHED ROSES. The best time to move an established rose is early spring before its leaves appear. It is possible, however, to transplant roses also when they are actively growing. ❶ To transplant a leafed-out rose, begin by cutting the canes back by one-half to two-thirds to reduce transplant shock. ❷ Use a spade to dig around the plant, lift it from the ground, and replant it in a new hole. The leaves will probably wilt. ❸ Keep the plant well-watered until it revives.

< 19 >

By late June or early July, depending on where you live, roses have produced their first flush of flowers. Your tasks are to cut them—to enjoy indoors in bouquets and to encourage continued bloom—and to keep the plants and leaves healthy and vigorous.

❶ CUT FLOWERS. For maximum flower production, snip just above a five-leaflet stem when cutting flowers for indoor arrangements.

❷ DEADHEAD. Remove spent flowers by cutting stems just above a five-leaflet leaf.

PEST WATCH. Keep an eye out for common pests such as aphids, slugs and snails, black spot, and Japanese beetles. ❸ Spray or pick off the bugs as needed. For more information about pest control, see pages 24 to 30.

WATER AND MULCH. Water roses if rainfall has been minimal. Mulch to reduce water loss, smother weeds, and keep soil cooler and more favorable for roots.

CONTINUE TO FEED. Repeat-blooming roses thrive with regular feeding. Feed them as directed on the plant food package.

PINCH OR DISBUD. You can control the size of your flowers by disbudding (removing all but one terminal bud). While this reduces the number of flowers on the bush, the ones remaining will be much larger. To yield more, but smaller, blooms, pinch out the center bud.

PRUNE AS NEEDED. Keep an eye out for damaged or diseased canes and clip them back to the ground. Suckers, or vigorous canes that grow from the root stock, usually show themselves in summer. Cut wildly growing suckers back to ground level too.

< **21** >

Rose Care: Fall and Winter

Once you feel the nip of fall in the air, your roses do too. They'll grow more slowly, gradually retreating into dormancy for the coming cold weather. Help them snuggle down for the winter by tackling a few easy winterizing chores.

❶ LEAVE HIPS TO RIPEN. Instead of cutting blooms off, let the last crop of flowers mature, fade, and develop hips—the fruit of the rose. This helps the plant become dormant, which increases its cold resistance. Hips also add color to winter's drab palette of browns and grays and will lure hungry birds to your garden.

TIDY UP THE GARDEN. Rake leaves and mulch away from the base of plants. Disease spores or insect eggs may hide there.

WRAP TREE ROSES. Set tall stakes around a tree rose and attach burlap to the stakes, creating a cage for protecting the rose over winter. ❷ Fill the cage, stuffing leaves or mulch between the burlap and the rose.

PROTECT GRAFTED ROSES FOR WINTER. Where temperatures drop to near 0°F, you'll need to protect the bud union from freezing. Set a cage around the plants, then fill it with fallen leaves or mulch. Where temperatures regularly drop below 0°F, grafted roses need greater protection. ❸ Place a cylinder—paper, cardboard, plastic, or metal—around the bush, and fill it with mulch or soil. In both cases, remove the mulch or soil in spring; work carefully to avoid breaking off new growth. Winter protection is not necessary where winters are mild (rarely colder than 25°F).

< 22 >

3

LOWER AND COVER CLIMBERS. Where temperatures dip below 0°F, remove climbing roses from their supports, lay the canes on the ground, and cover them with leaves or soil.

PRUNE AS NEEDED. If heavy snow or ice breaks thin branches on unmulched plants, a light pruning during winter is a good idea.

ORDER ROSES FOR NEXT SEASON. Browse mail-order catalogs for roses and place your order now for planting next spring.

< 23 >

Rumor has it that it's difficult to grow healthy roses. Not true! Although diseases, insects, and other inhabitants of the natural world may inflict harm upon roses, few of these are devastating. In fact, most pests abandon plants when environmental conditions change. Maintain healthy roses and be a good steward of the environment by practicing integrated pest management, or IPM. The main focus of IPM is prevention, with chemical controls employed as a last resort.

Give roses a healthy start

Select strong plants with proven resilience to the weather extremes and stressors of your region's climate. Select pest-resistant varieties. (Although not immune to insects and diseases, these roses have fewer problems and are less susceptible to specific pests.)

BE SURE TO PLANT ROSES WHERE they will receive at least six hours of sun. Not only do roses grow the strongest in sun, but in the warmth of the sun, leaves dry quickly, which helps prevent fungal diseases such as black spot and powdery mildew. Water plants early in the day for the same reason.

SPACE ROSES 2 to 3 feet apart so air can move around the plants, which helps ward off disease by keeping foliage dry. Prune to allow light and air to reach the center of the plants.

PLANT ROSES AWAY FROM WATER-HOGGING trees and shrubs so they'll have a better chance of absorbing enough moisture.

INSTEAD OF PLANTING AN ALL-ROSE GARDEN, intermingle roses among a variety of plants. Diverse planting reduces the spread of disease and attracts beneficial insects.

< 24 >

Promote healthy conditions

Remember: Healthy, vigorous plants resist infestation. Once established, keep your roses going strong with consistent, basic care.

WATER AND FEED roses regularly. Roses react adversely to the stressors of extreme thirst or malnutrition. Feed the soil and plants by supplementing plant food with compost and rotted manure to provide nutrients while improving the soil structure.

PRUNE ROSES AS NEEDED, lopping off parts affected by cane borers (look for brown swollen canes that house developing insect larvae) or canker (a dark, swollen area on canes).

PROVIDE A CLEAN ENVIRONMENT. Diseases and other garden pests spread by way of gardeners' hands, shoes, and tools. When working around afflicted plants, prevent the spread of disease by cleaning tools, gloves, and shoes before tending healthy plants. Also, avoid working around roses when foliage is wet. This, too, could spread disease.

What to do when pests strike

- Catch diseases and insects in their early stages for easier control. Check plants regularly for signs of trouble.

- Learn to identify disease and insect problems so that you can determine how to best handle them. Ortho's *Home Gardener's Problem Solver* is a great resource.

- If a pest population is small and the damage is minimal, pick off insects such as Japanese beetles or munching caterpillars; squish them or drop them in a container of soapy water.

- For localized problems, spot treatment with a ready-to-use product provides quick, easy, and effective control. This approach balances effective pest control with protecting the environment.

- Remember: There are no flawless roses. A perfect rose is one that gives you immense pleasure and requires only a little care in return.

Black spot

PROBLEM

❶ Circular black spots with fringed yellow margins appear on the upper surfaces of the leaves in the spring. The tissue around the spot or the entire leaf may turn yellow, and the infected leaves may drop prematurely. Severely infected plants may lose all of their leaves by midsummer. Flower production is often reduced and quality is poor.

SOLUTION

Black spot is a fungus that is a severe problem in areas that commonly experience high humidity or excessive rain in spring and summer. Splashing water enables it to spread from plant to plant. Avoid overhead watering.

Spray with Ortho Garden Disease Control or Orthenex Insect & Disease Control. Repeat the treatment at intervals of 7 to 10 days for as long as the weather remains wet. Refrain from spraying during hot, dry spells in summer. Prune off infected canes. In the fall, rake up and destroy the fallen leaves. After pruning plants during the dormant season, spray with a lime-sulfur solution. The following spring, when new growth starts, begin the spray program again.

Powdery mildew

PROBLEM

❷ A layer of powdery, grayish-white material covers young leaves, young twigs, and flower buds. Infected leaves may be distorted and curled; they may turn yellow or purplish and drop off. The mildew can stunt new growth and kill young canes. Infected flower buds don't open properly. In late summer, tiny black dots may appear scattered over the powdery covering like ground pepper.

< 26 >

SOLUTION

Powdery mildew is a common plant disease caused by a fungus. It is one of the most widespread and serious diseases of roses. Powdery mildew may occur on roses anytime during the growing season when rainfall is low or absent, temperatures are 70° to 80°F, nighttime relative humidity is high, and daytime relative humidity is low. In areas where there is high rainfall in spring and summer, control may not be needed until the drier months of late summer.

Apply Ortho Garden Disease Control or Ortho Orthenex Insect & Disease Control at the first sign of mildew. Repeat the spray at intervals of 7 to 10 days if mildew reappears. Rake up and destroy infected leaves in the fall. If powdery mildew is a serious problem in your area, be sure to select resistant varieties.

Rust

PROBLEM

❸ Yellow to brown spots up to ¼ inch in diameter appear on the upper surfaces of leaves, starting in the spring or late fall. The disease affects leaves closest to the flower first. On the undersides of leaves are spots or blotches containing a red, orange, or black powdery material that can be scraped off. Infected leaves may become twisted and dry and drop off the plant, or they may remain attached. Rust can also infect twigs. Severely infected plants lack vigor.

SOLUTION

Rust is caused by any of several species of fungi that infest only rose plants. Wind spreads the orange fungal spores to rose leaves. With moisture and moderate temperatures the spores enter the leaves. Rake up and destroy infected leaves in the fall. Prune off and destroy infected twigs. Plant resistant varieties.

At the first sign of rust, pick off and destroy the infected leaves and spray with Ortho Garden Disease Control or Ortho Orthenex Insect & Disease Control. Repeat at intervals of 7 to 14 days for as long as conditions that spread the disease—ample moisture and moderate temperatures—persist.

< 27 >

Common Insects and Other Pests

For best results in controlling insects, use insecticides and miticides at the first sign of infestation. Spraying to prevent attack rarely works, is costly, and can destroy natural predators and other beneficial insects. Waiting too long to spray can let pest populations build up.

Some rose growers prefer not to use any chemicals in their gardens and instead rely on natural predators to control destructive insects. Helpful species include ladybugs, green lacewings, praying mantids, parasitic wasps, and predatory mites. The drawback to these insects is that once they have eaten the pests in your garden, they will move on to other gardens in search of food. Their overall effectiveness may not last long.

Flower thrips

PROBLEM

❶ Young leaves appear distorted, and foliage may have yellow flecks. Flower buds become deformed and often fail to open. Brown streaks and red spots may cover petals of open blossoms, especially those of white or light-colored varieties. If you pull apart a deformed or streaked flower and shake it over white paper, you will likely see tiny yellow or brown insects fall out.

SOLUTION

Thrips are difficult to control because they continuously migrate to roses from other plants. Immediately remove and destroy infected buds and blooms. Spray with Ortho Systemic Insect Killer or Ortho Bug-B-Gon Multi-Purpose Insect Killer Ready-Spray three times at intervals of 7 to 10 days.

< 28 >

Japanese beetles

PROBLEM

2 Adult Japanese beetles leave behind chewed-up leaves and destroyed flowers and flower buds. Japanese beetles are ⅜-inch-long metallic green beetles with copper-brown wing covers. They have small circular tufts of white hairs on the edge of the wings, and a pair of tufts at the tip of their abdomen. These white tufts distinguish Japanese beetles from similar beetles.

Japanese beetles usually feed in groups, starting at the top of a plant and working downward, and prefer plants exposed to direct sunlight. A single beetle does not eat much; group-feeding causes the severe damage.

SOLUTION

3 Control Japanese beetles with Ortho Bug-B-Gon Japanese Beetle Killer, Ortho Bug-B-Gon MAX Insect Killer for Lawns, Ortho Systemic Insect Killer, or Ortho Bug-B-Gon Garden & Landscape Insect Killer.

Leafhoppers

PROBLEM

4 Whitish insects, up to ½ inch long, hop and fly away quickly when the plant is touched. Affected leaves have white stippling. Severely infested plants may die. Rose leafhopper is a serious pest of roses and apples and several ornamental trees.

SOLUTION

Spray with Ortho Systemic Insect Killer or Ortho Bug-B-Gon Multi-Purpose Insect Killer Concentrate when you first notice damage. Cover the lower surfaces of leaves thoroughly with the spray. Repeat if the plant becomes reinfested.

< 29 >

Rose aphids

PROBLEM

④ Tiny (⅛-inch), green or pink, soft-bodied insects cluster on leaves, stems, and developing buds. Heavy infestation can deform flower buds and prevent them from opening properly. A shiny, sticky substance often coats the leaves and black, sooty mold may grow on the sticky substance. You may also see ants.

Rose aphids do little damage in small numbers, but they are extremely prolific and can rapidly build up to damaging numbers during the growing season.

SOLUTION

Spray with Ortho Systemic Insect Killer, Ortho Bug-B-Gon Multi-Purpose Insect Killer Ready-to-Use, or an insecticidal soap when you notice clusters of aphids. Repeat the treatment if the plant becomes reinfested. Ladybug adults and larvae aid control as they feed on the aphids.

Rose borers

PROBLEM

⑤ Large canes wilt and die. Affected stems may be swollen at the base. Cutting across the damaged stem reveals a hollow core. You see white to yellowish grubs after peeling back the bark or slicing lengthwise through the stem.

SOLUTION

Prune and destroy infested stems, cutting until you find the borer or the end of the hollowed core. If borers attack your roses every year, immediately seal all cuts with Ortho Pruning Sealer. Old, weakened, or stressed plants are most susceptible to borer damage, however, some borers attack healthy plants. Keeping plants in good health helps prevent problems.

< 30 >

HYBRID TEA ROSES

HYBRID TEA BASICS

OVERALL FORM: Upright plants with flowers topping long single stems.

SIZE: 3–5' tall, 3–4' wide.

BLOOM TIME: Off and on all summer.

FRAGRANCE: Many are scented.

ZONES: 5–9 (with winter protection in Zone 4).

> Flower colors span all except true blue and black, including bicolors and blends.

> Plants need ample water and plant food.

HYBRID TEA ROSES with their classic elegance, vigor, and repeat blooming are the most popular group of roses grown today. Gardeners prize their high-centered, sculptural blooms that make wonderful cut flowers. The plants typically produce one flower at the end of each long stem at regular intervals of 35 to 45 days. Cutting the blooms and removing spent flowers—or deadheading—induces the next flowering cycle.

When they were first cultivated, hybrid teas had large fragrant blooms and a weakness for disease. In subsequent decades, breeders sought to bring disease resistance and cold hardiness to the shrubs. The hybridizers succeeded to some extent, but many of the roses they developed lost the fragrance of their ancestors. Today's plant breeders keep the desirability of scent at the forefront of their efforts to attain the perfect rose.

Grow hybrid teas in a cut-flower border or add them to a perennial border for a punch of color. Their upright habit makes them best suited for growing with companion plants (see page 90) that will mask their occasional leggy appearance.

< 32 >

Care: Pruning tips

Annual pruning is essential to the health, vigor, and form of hybrid teas. Follow these spring pruning steps and deadhead throughout the growing season to encourage repeat blooms on your hybrid tea rose.

❶ Begin pruning in early spring, removing all damaged, weak, or crossing canes. Select the three or four newest and healthiest of the remaining canes and cut the rest flush with the bud union, using pruning shears or a saw if necessary. ❷ Prune the remaining canes to 12 to 18 inches tall, as measured from the bud union.

Deadhead by cutting the flower back to the nearest five-leaflet leaf where the stem is at least as large as the diameter of a pencil. This will spur the plant to create new flowers.

Notes

_____
_____
_____
_____
_____
_____
_____
_____
_____
_____
_____
_____
_____
_____
_____
_____

< 33 >

HYBRID TEA CULTIVARS

'INGRID BERGMAN'

'ELLE'

'MEMORIAL DAY' 'LOVE AND PEACE'

There are more than 10,000 **HYBRID TEA ROSE** cultivars. When selecting plants for your landscape, try some of these winning selections or grow others with notable disease resistance and vigor.

'Elle'
HARDY TO ZONE 6 • PINK FLOWERS • SIZE: 3 TO 4 FEET TALL AND WIDE • GOOD DISEASE RESISTANCE • INTENSE SCENT • AARS WINNER
Strong points of 'Elle' include its spicy, citrus fragrance and high-centered classic rosebud. Its shell-pink flowers with deep yellow undertones are 4 to 5 inches wide. The dark, glossy foliage provides a nice contrast to the soft, nonfading flower and offers above average disease tolerance to mildew and black spot.

< 34 >

'Ingrid Bergman'

HARDY TO ZONE 5 • RED FLOWER • SIZE: 2 TO 3 FEET TALL AND WIDE • MODERATE SCENT • GOOD DISEASE RESISTANCE • ARS RATING: 7.2

Classic deep red flowers make 'Ingrid Bergman' a favorite hybrid tea rose all over the world. The flowers spiral open from long, elegant buds that are almost black. The fully-double flowers stand up well to rain. This healthy, hardy rose features shiny leaves and crimson new growth.

'Love and Peace'

HARDY TO ZONE 6 • YELLOW AND CRIMSON FLOWERS • SIZE: 6 FEET TALL AND 3 FEET WIDE • MODERATE SCENT • EXCELLENT DISEASE RESISTANCE • AARS WINNER

A seedling of the famous 'Peace' rose developed in 1945, this 2002 introduction has buff yellow petals with crimson edges. The plant flowers freely, even in hot climates, and is covered with vigorous, healthy dark green glittering foliage. 'Love and Peace' has a lovely habit that complements perennial gardens and shrub borders.

'Memorial Day'

HARDY TO ZONE 6 • PINK FLOWER • SIZE: 4 FEET TALL AND WIDE • INTENSE SCENT • EXCELLENT DISEASE RESISTANCE • AARS WINNER

This medium-tall, upright, and bushy variety features very large, full, spiraled blooms with more than 50 petals per flower. A lavender wash accents clear pink flowers evolving from pointed and ovoid buds that open to 5 inches in diameter. Long cutting stems beautifully clothed with rich green foliage set off the large blossoms.

With its classic, strong damask rose fragrance, a single 'Memorial Day' rose can fill an entire room with sweet rose perfume. A vigorous and productive grower, 'Memorial Day' is disease resistant and is an excellent selection for hot weather climates.

More great hybrid teas

'BARBRA STREISAND' (lavender with purple margins)
'DOUBLE DELIGHT' (cream with strawberry markings)
'MISTER LINCOLN' (deep red)
'SUNSET CELEBRATION' (apricot)
'UNCLE JOE' (large red)

Notes

< 35 >

GRANDIFLORAS

GRANDIFLORA ROSE

GRANDIFLORA BASICS

OVERALL FORM: Tall plants with clusters of flowers on a long stem

SIZE: 4–6' tall

FRAGRANCE: Some are scented.

ZONES: 5–9

>Generally, plants are hardy.

>Flower colors include all hues except true blue and black.

>They are good for screening and for cut flowers.

Tall and strong, **GRANDIFLORAS** exhibit the best traits of their parents: the classic flower form of hybrid tea and the hardiness, continuous flowering, and clustered blooms of floribunda. The class was created in the United States to accommodate 'Queen Elizabeth', considered the prototype of the perfect grandiflora when it was introduced in 1954.

These are excellent landscape roses that grow to 6 feet tall; one long stem erupts in an entire bouquet of large roses. Now widely termed cluster-flowered roses, they're useful for cut flowers as well as for background color in the garden. The vigorous shrubs are popular as hedges and screens. They are typically disease resistant and cold hardy.

< 36 >

Care: Harvesting roses for bouquets

Grandifloras, along with hybrid teas, have excellent flowers for cutting. Enjoy petal-packed, fragrant bouquets with these tips.

❶ Cut roses that are just beginning to open. A cut rose will last longer if it is cut when the flower is not completely open.

Harvest roses late in the afternoon when the plant is brimming with sugars and nutrients.

With pruning shears, cut stems at a 45-degree angle just above the first five-leaflet leaf below the flower. If stems are less thick than a pencil, cut further down the stem. Place the cut stems in a bucket of water immediately.

❷ Before arranging flowers, recut the stems at a slant underwater. This reopens the cut and permits maximum water absorption.

Notes

_____
_____
_____
_____
_____
_____
_____
_____
_____
_____
_____
_____
_____
_____

< 37 >

'CHERRY PARFAIT'

'GOLD MEDAL'

'QUEEN ELIZABETH'

'HI NEIGHBOR'

Whether you grow **GRANDIFLORAS** for their impressive flower clusters or for their stately size, you'll enjoy these winning cultivars. Plant three or four plants for lovely mixed-rose bouquets.

'About Face'

HARDY TO ZONE 5 • YELLOW AND ORANGE FLOWER • SIZE: 4 FEET TALL AND WIDE • MODERATE SCENT • EXCELLENT DISEASE RESISTANCE • AARS WINNER

'About Face' is a novel "backwards" bicolor, with a light shade of deep golden yellow on the inside of the petals and a darker bronzy orange-red on the backside. This vigorous plant yields long stems with full, old-fashioned blossoms. The flowers, up to 5 inches in diameter, have a mild fresh apple fragrance and are complemented by lush, clean green leaves.

< 38 >

'Cherry Parfait'

HARDY TO ZONE 6 • RED AND WHITE FLOWERS • SIZE: 5 FEET TALL AND WIDE • LIGHT SCENT • GOOD DISEASE RESISTANCE • AARS WINNER

'Cherry Parfait' takes maximum advantage of its shrubby appearance as a backdrop for its showy blossoms. Its white petals with a broad red edge are a treat for the eyes. The plant's loose habit makes it a good companion for perennials and shrubbery. Seemingly always in bloom, this bicolor rose accented by dark foliage is attractive throughout the season and also is an effective container plant.

'Gold Medal'

HARDY TO ZONE 6 • YELLOW FLOWERS • SIZE: 5 FEET TALL BY 3 FEET WIDE • LIGHT SCENT • GOOD DISEASE RESISTANCE • ARS RATING: 8.5

One of the best yellow roses in any group, 'Gold Medal' has elegant orange-yellow buds that slowly open to reveal rich golden flowers that fade to pale yellow and eventually to white as they age. This tall, upright bush bears long-stemmed flowers singly or in clusters of up to seven. It's an excellent grandiflora for hot climates.

'Hi Neighbor'

HARDY TO ZONE 5 • DARK PINK FLOWER • SIZE: 5 FEET TALL BY 4 FEET WIDE • MILD SCENT • MODERATE DISEASE RESISTANCE

The large dark pink flowers of 'Hi Neighbor' are so full that they tend to hang down under their own weight. The flowers bloom singly and in clusters of up to five, and the plant reblooms regularly until the first frost. Plants grow well in both cool and hot climates.

More great grandifloras

'FAME!' (bright pink)
'LOVE' (red with white reverse)
'OCTOBERFEST' (deep crimson)
'QUEEN ELIZABETH' (pink)
'TOURNAMENT OF ROSES' (beige-pink)

Notes

_____
_____
_____
_____
_____
_____
_____

< 39 >

'CHARISMA' FLORIBUNDA ROSE

FLORIBUNDA BASICS

OVERALL FORM: Mostly upright-growing shrubs that produce clusters of flowers.	
SIZE: 2–4' tall and wide.	
BLOOM TIME: All season.	
FRAGRANCE: Many have fragrance.	
ZONES: 4–9	

>Flower colors range from white and pink to yellow, red, and striped or bicolors.

FLORIBUNDAS are exceptional as landscape and bedding roses. They require little care and bloom profusely all season. The flowers, slightly smaller than those of hybrid teas, occur in clusters and are single, semidouble, or double.

Floribundas are hardier and more disease resistant than hybrid teas. They need winter protection in cold climates.

Their compact growth habit makes them ideal for a mass display of color in a hedge or edging, depending on the size of the garden. Plant them in front of tall, leggy roses such as grandifloras. Add a floribunda to a perennial garden for a reliable patch of color. Plant floribundas in pots to create spots of concentrated, lasting color.

< 40 >

Care: Planting, pruning, and caring for a floribunda hedge

1 Create a blooming fence with a row of floribunda roses. Follow these pruning suggestions for a dense and abundantly flowering floribunda hedge.

FOR A HEALTHY, DENSE HEDGE, plant floribundas 3 feet apart. Resist the urge to plant them closer together. Planting close together reduces air circulation and promotes disease growth.

2 Spread a 2- to 3-inch layer of organic mulch around each rose in the entire hedgerow. While helping conserve soil moisture, the mulch will inhibit weeds from sprouting up between your roses.

MAKE WATERING EASY by winding a drip hose through the hedge planting. Attach a timer to the hose so all you have to remember to do is switch on the water.

3 **IN EARLY SPRING,** prune away dead, diseased, or weak canes.

SELECT FIVE OR SIX OF THE NEWEST, healthiest remaining canes and remove the rest, cutting flush with the bud union.

TRIM REMAINING CANES back to about 24 inches above the bud union.

Notes

_____

_____

_____

_____

_____

_____

_____

_____

< **41** >

'HONEY PERFUME'

'HOT COCOA'

'BETTY PRIOR'   'ICEBERG'

FLORIBUNDAS are excellent plants for a low-maintenance landscape. Plan for nonstop flowering from spring to fall with these floribunda selections.

'Betty Prior'
HARDY TO ZONE 5 • PINK FLOWERS • SIZE: 3 FEET TALL AND WIDE • LIGHT SCENT • GOOD DISEASE RESISTANCE • ARS RATING: 8.2
This tough, enduring rose has deep pink flowers that fade to a ghostly white as they age. The dogwoodlike flowers bloom in clusters of five to 15 and are lightly scented. The upright vigorous plant is disease resistant and excellent for mass plantings.

< 42 >

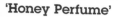

'Honey Perfume'

HARDY TO ZONE 6 • APRICOT FLOWERS • SIZE: 3 FEET TALL BY 2 FEET WIDE • INTENSE SCENT • GOOD DISEASE RESISTANCE • AARS WINNER

'Honey Perfume' is an upright and well-branched floribunda with apricot-yellow blooms. Pointed, shapely buds open to reveal beautiful 4-inch blooms nestled among glossy dark green foliage that accentuates their color. 'Honey Perfume' has a great spicy scent and very good resistance to disease, including rust and powdery mildew.

'Hot Cocoa'

HARDY TO ZONE 6 • AUBURN FLOWERS • SIZE: 4 FEET TALL AND WIDE • LIGHT SCENT • EXCELLENT DISEASE RESISTANCE • AARS WINNER

'Hot Cocoa' is a novel brownish-orange floribunda with a smokey wash on the top of the petals and a deep rusty orange on the underside. The 4-inch flowers are moderately sweet-smelling and hold their color well. 'Hot Cocoa' is a seedling of the popular and trouble-free floribunda 'Playboy'. This vigorous rose tolerates heat and is disease resistant.

'Iceberg'

HARDY TO ZONE 5 • WHITE FLOWERS • SIZE: 3 TO 4 FEET TALL AND WIDE • MILD SCENT • GOOD DISEASE RESISTANCE • ARS RATING: 8.6

Throughout the season 'Iceberg' bears attractive pure white flowers that appear in open, airy sprays at the ends of long stems. Its foliage is lush, glossy, and always healthy. In cool climates blooms can display an occasional flush of pink. 'Iceberg' is grown as a standard, climber, or handsome rounded bush.

More great floribundas

'BETTY BOOP' (ivory-yellow with red edging)
'CHARISMA' (scarlet-and-yellow)
'EUREKA' (yellow)
'FRENCH LACE' (white)
'LIVIN' EASY' (apricot-orange)
'PLAYBOY' (scarlet-orange with a yellow center)

Notes

_____
_____
_____
_____
_____
_____

< **43** >

'MARGO KOSTER', 'DICK KOSTER', AND 'MOTHER'S DAY' POLYANTHA ROSES

POLYANTHA BASICS

OVERALL FORM: Mostly compact, rounded plants with clusters of small (1-inch) flowers.

SIZE: 18–36" tall.

BLOOM TIME: Most repeat-bloom all season.

FRAGRANCE: Some have light fragrance.

ZONES: 4–10

>Polyanthas withstand heat better than most roses.

>Flower colors include pink, red, orange, yellow, and white.

POLYANTHAS are perfect for beds and low hedges, typically growing knee-high in compact forms that produce small, clustered flowers from early summer until fall. Polyanthas' general hardiness, durability, and usefulness in the landscape make up for the lack of fragrance in some varieties.

Plant polyanthas as ground covers, as edging along a border, or as foundation shrubs. Smaller varieties thrive in containers. Train taller ones to climb trellises, or let them wind their way through shrubs or perennial borders.

< **44** >

Care: Pruning polyanthas

Polyanthas are hardy plants that, like many old garden and shrub roses, seldom suffer winterkill. For this reason, prune them more as you would old garden and species roses than hybrid teas, floribundas, and grandifloras.

IF POLYANTHAS ARE NOT OVERGROWN, trim only to remove old, damaged, or diseased canes.

IF THEY ARE OVERGROWN, prune them in early spring to about half their former height, and remove about half of the oldest, largest canes. For the best look, leave them on the bushy side.

Growing polyanthas with perennials

Polyanthas' hardiness and adaptability make them good candidates for planting in the perennial border. Polyanthas are eye-catching when they are allowed to sprawl with abandon through spikes and spires of blooming plants. For an attractive, healthy polyantha rose and perennial garden, keep these tips in mind.

PRUNE polyanthas in early spring before the perennials emerge. The perennial bed can get very dense by midspring; so make a point to prune before the perennials emerge.

1 PLANT A MIX of ground covers, medium, and tall plants around polyantha roses for a cottage garden look. Aim to add a variety of shapes and textures to the planting bed.

CLOSE QUARTERS, like those in a dense perennial bed, create conditions right for the development of powdery mildew. If the disease strikes, thin nearby plants to promote good air circulation.

Notes

< 45 >

'CHINA DOLL'

'MARIE PAVIÉ'

'CÉCILE BRÜNNER'

'THE FAIRY'

Floriferous, low-growing plants, **POLYANTHAS** make great hedges and edging plants. Plant a few of these beloved bloomers.

'Cécile Brünner'

HARDY TO ZONE 6 • PINK FLOWERS • SIZE: 3 FEET TALL AND WIDE • MODERATE SCENT • GOOD DISEASE RESISTANCE • ARS RATING: 8.4

Each of the tiny flowers that cover 'Cécile Brünner' resembles a miniature hybrid tea. The slender, pointed buds open in clusters of 10 to 25 to reveal perfect light pink flowers. Nicknamed the "sweetheart rose" in generations past, 'Cécile Brünner' is covered with lightly scented blooms from spring until frost. Look for equally excellent 'White Cécile Brünner', 'Climbing Cécile Brünner', and 'Spray Cécile Brünner'.

< 46 >

'China Doll'

HARDY TO ZONE 5 • PINK FLOWERS • SIZE: 2 FEET TALL BY 3 FEET WIDE • LIGHT SCENT • EXCELLENT DISEASE RESISTANCE

The ruffled edges of 'China Doll' blooms give it a playful, informal appearance. Small, semidouble pink flowers open in large clusters above dark green leaves. The flowers are long-lasting and repeat so quickly that 'China Doll' seems always to be in flower. This easy-to-grow plant tolerates poor soil and is useful for containers and as an edging plant. 'Weeping China Doll' and 'Climbing China Doll' differ from 'China Doll' only in growth habit.

'Marie Pavié'

HARDY TO ZONE 6 • WHITE FLOWERS • SIZE: 2 FEET TALL BY 2 FEET WIDE • INTENSE SCENT • MODERATE DISEASE RESISTANCE • ARS RATING: 8.9

'Marie Pavié' has classic pointed buds that unfurl into pale double blooms. It bears delicately fragrant flowers in clusters of five to 20, well above the foliage. The plant is vigorous, compact, thornless, and almost perpetually in flower.

'The Fairy'

HARDY TO ZONE 6 • PINK FLOWERS • SIZE: 2 FEET TALL BY 4 FEET WIDE • MODERATE SCENT • EXCELLENT DISEASE RESISTANCE • ARS RATING: 8.7

The world's most popular and widely grown polyantha, 'The Fairy' is one of the easiest roses to grow. Its tiny flowers open as a cheerful pink and fade to pale pink and eventually almost white. The clusters of 10 to 40 flowers unfurl in summer and continue blooming well into autumn. Petite, glossy leaves complement the flowers. 'The Fairy' is an excellent ground cover or edging plant.

More great polyanthas

'ALBERICH' (red)
'ELSE POULSEN' (pink)
'LA MARNE' (pink)
'MARGO KOSTER' (pink)
'PERLE d'OR' (salmon-pink)

Notes
_____
_____
_____
_____

< **47** >

'HAPPY TRAILS' MINIATURE ROSE

MINIATURE BASICS

OVERALL FORM: Petite plants with leaves and flowers in proportion to their size.

SIZE: 6–24" tall; climbers to 6'.

BLOOM TIME: All summer and into fall.

FRAGRANCE: Some are fragrant.

ZONES: 4–9.

> Flowers include all colors and bicolors.

> Miniature roses work well in containers and as edging.

Scarcely known before the 1930s, **MINIATURE ROSES** now foster widespread popularity for their petite charms. As dwarf plants, with flowers and foliage in proportion to their size, miniature roses are available in a wide assortment of colors, flower forms, and growth habits. Although some climb to 6 feet tall and others sprawl to 2 feet wide, some hybrids grow just 6 to 18 inches tall.

Ideal for pots, hanging baskets, and windowsills, miniatures also make excellent edging plants and are just the right touch for a small space. Surprisingly winter hardy, they are profuse bloomers that require little care. Gather handfuls of miniature blooms for a vase and enjoy them indoors too.

You might encounter the term "miniflora" when searching for miniature roses. Minifloras are between miniatures and floribundas in bloom size and foliage. The American Rose Society adopted this new class in 1999.

< **48** >

Care: Growing Miniatures

Miniature roses thrive when given the same
care as full-size roses, with a few exceptions.
Follow these easy tips for growing healthy
diminutive beauties.

❶ FEED PLANTS REGULARLY. Miniatures
bloom constantly from summer until fall. Give
these heavy feeders a nutrient boost by
applying Miracle-Gro Shake 'n Feed
Continuous Release Rose Plant Food every
three months and Miracle-Gro Water Soluble
Rose Plant Food every few weeks.

❷ PRUNE AS NEEDED. Encourage miniatures
to repeat bloom by deadheading spent flowers.
Prune faded flowers back to the nearest five-
leaflet leaf. In spring, prune away dead and
damaged wood.

OVERWINTER WITH MULCH. Although
miniature roses are notably hardy, in northern
climates they benefit from a 6- to 8-inch layer
of insulating mulch. Cover plants with loose
mulch such as wood chips, hay, or evergreen
boughs after the first frost. In spring, remove
the mulch when daytime temperatures
regularly reach 50°F.

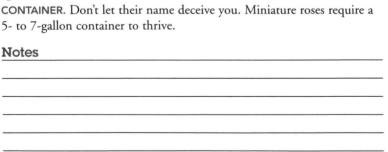

**❸ PLANT MINIATURES IN A LARGE
CONTAINER.** Don't let their name deceive you. Miniature roses require a
5- to 7-gallon container to thrive.

Notes

_____

_____

_____

_____

_____

_____

_____

< **49** >

'BLACK JADE'

'RAINBOW'S END'

'GOURMET POPCORN'   'SUN SPRINKLES'

MINIATURE ROSES are a versatile group. Whether they are grown in containers or used as a burst of color in a flower bed, the following tiny treasures are sure to delight.

'Black Jade'
HARDY TO ZONE 5 • DARK RED • SIZE: 2 FEET TALL AND WIDE • MINIMAL SCENT • MODERATE DISEASE RESISTANCE • ARS RATING: 8.1
Some rose growers claim that 'Black Jade' is the deepest red of all roses. It is certainly the darkest miniature rose, and its flowers are exquisitely formed like petite hybrid teas. Although the flowers are scentless, the plant's abundant, novel blooms make it an excellent addition to any garden. In hot climates grow 'Black Jade' in partial sun, where it keeps its color better.

< 50 >

'Gourmet Popcorn'

HARDY TO ZONE 4 • WHITE FLOWERS • SIZE: 2 TO 3 FEET TALL AND WIDE • LIGHT SCENT • GOOD DISEASE RESISTANCE • ARS RATING: 8.7

Pure white flowers blanket 'Gourmet Popcorn' throughout summer. The massive clusters of flowers have a light fragrance and are accompanied by disease-resistant dark green foliage. 'Gourmet Popcorn' is prized for its ease of use in the landscape—it looks good in containers, in hanging baskets, as a border plant, and as a standard tree.

'Rainbow's End'

HARDY TO ZONE 5 • YELLOW AND RED FLOWERS • SIZE: 1 TO 1½ FEET TALL AND WIDE • LIGHT SCENT • MODERATE DISEASE RESISTANCE • ARS RATING: 8.8

Petite hybrid-tea-shaped blooms open rich yellow and then slowly turn crimson until the flower is almost completely red. The scentless blossoms mature at different rates to create a tapestry of color. The compact, low-growing bush is ideal for containers and borders.

'Sun Sprinkles'

HARDY TO ZONE 6 • YELLOW FLOWERS • SIZE: 3 FEET TALL BY 2 FEET WIDE • LIGHT SCENT • EXCELLENT DISEASE RESISTANCE • ARS RATING: 7.9

'Sun Sprinkles' bears long-lasting bright golden flowers that fade to pale yellow. The flowers, which bloom singly and in clusters, shine thanks to the plant's dark green foliage. Great miniature rose for edging. This miniature has excellent disease resistance.

More great miniatures

'BABY LOVE' (yellow)
'MAGIC CAROUSEL' (creamy white petals edged with pinkish red)
'MINNIE PEARL' (creamy white)
'SANTA CLAUS' (deep scarlet)
'SCENTSATIONAL' (mauve)

Notes

_____
_____
_____
_____
_____
_____
_____

< 51 >

CLIMBING ROSES

CLIMBING ROSE

CLIMBING BASICS

OVERALL FORM:
Vigorous canes, need initial support but eventually will climb on their own.

SIZE: 6–20'

BLOOM TIME: Summer; many repeat into fall.

FRAGRANCE: Some are fragrant.

ZONES: 4–9 (with winter protection in Zone 4).

>Blooms come in a wide range of colors.

Most **CLIMBING ROSES** are either large-flowering or cluster-flowering variations of bush-type roses. These vigorous plants produce canes that reach 6 to 20 feet in height. Depending on the variety, they bloom once a year or throughout the growing season.

Climbers make outstanding accents, clambering over trellises, arbors, pergolas, walls, or fences. They do an outstanding job of masking an unsightly chain link or barbed-wire fence. Unlike vines with tendrils, roses need help to climb and cling to a support. During a plant's first few summers in the landscape, the canes must be trained to climb. Loosely tie the canes to the support, gently guiding them in a horizontal direction to encourage more bloom. For more information on training a climbing rose to a support, to page 72.

Care: Pruning Climbers

Because climbers bloom on the previous year's growth (old wood), they are pruned differently than bush roses. Follow these steps for pruning climbing roses.

IN EARLY SPRING prune away dead or damaged canes. ❶ Also remove extra-long or misshapen canes. Leave all other pruning until after the plants bloom. ❷ Tie the canes so that they are horizontal; this will improve blooming.

AFTER THE FIRST FLUSH of blooms fade, remove the oldest canes to make room for new growth. Also thin out dense growth.

REMOVE SPENT FLOWERS to encourage the plant to rebloom.

Overwintering Climbers

Overwintering tender climbing roses is a time-consuming task. For easy overwintering chores, plant roses that are hardy in your climate and simply mound 12 inches of soil around the base. If you have to overwinter a tender climbing rose, follow these steps.

❸ After the first frost, remove the rose from its support. Trim the canes so they are easy to gather into a bundle. Using twine, tie the canes into a vertical bundle. Tip the plant over and tie it down for security. Mound up the base of the plant with soil and cover the plant with leaves. You could also wrap the bundle with burlap, canvas, or a similar fabric (never plastic).

Notes

_____
_____
_____
_____
_____
_____

< 53 >

'BLAZE'

'HENRY KELSEY'

'AMERICA'

'NEW DAWN'

Dress up an arbor, pergola, or garage wall with a **CLIMBING ROSE**. Count on these no-fuss, repeat-blooming climbers to add a splash.

'America'

HARDY TO ZONE 6 • CORAL-PINK FLOWER • SIZE: 10 FEET TALL BY 6½ FEET WIDE • STRONG SCENT • GOOD DISEASE RESISTANCE • AARS WINNER • ARS RATING: 8.3

You are likely to smell 'America' before you see this climber. A strong, sweet scent permeates the air when the salmon-pink flowers are in bloom. The flowers resemble those of classic hybrid teas. This neat, sturdy, upright plant grows moderately and reblooms intermittently throughout the season.

< 54 >

'Blaze'

HARDY TO ZONE 5 • RED FLOWERS • SIZE: 13 FEET TALL BY 8 FEET WIDE • LIGHT SCENT • EXCELLENT DISEASE RESISTANCE • ARS RATING: 7.2

This easy-to-grow climber has an impressive initial flush of bright red flowers all along the length of its canes. Smaller flushes of bloom follow later in the season. The blooms have a light tea fragrance. The plant's large green leaves shrug off disease well.

'Henry Kelsey'

HARDY TO ZONE 3 • CRIMSON FLOWERS • SIZE: 8 FEET TALL BY 6 FEET WIDE • INTENSE FRAGRANCE • MODERATE DISEASE RESISTANCE

One of the hardiest of all climbers, 'Henry Kelsey' easily withstands Zone 3 winters. It has clusters of semidouble dark red flowers highlighted with bright yellow stamens. Repeat blooming 'Henry Kelsey' has a spicy fragrance and eye-catching glossy green foliage.

'New Dawn'

HARDY TO ZONE 4 • LIGHT PINK FLOWERS • SIZE: 13 FEET TALL BY 6½ FEET WIDE • MODERATE FRAGRANCE • EXCELLENT DISEASE RESISTANCE • ARS RATING: 8.6

Clusters of large, full light pink flowers decorate sweetly scented 'New Dawn' all season long. This champion bloomer is constantly bedecked with flowers when planted in full sun and watered and fed regularly. The glossy dark foliage is highly disease resistant.

More great climbers

'ALTISSIMO' (red)

'FOURTH OF JULY' (red and white)

'GOLDEN SHOWERS' (yellow)

'JOSEPH'S COAT' (yellow and red mix)

WHITE LADY BANK'S ROSE *(ROSA BANKSIAE BANKSIAE)* (white)

Notes

_____

_____

_____

_____

_____

_____

_____

_____

< 55 >

'SEVILLIANA' SHRUB ROSE

SHRUB BASICS	
OVERALL FORM:	
Compact or sprawling. Single or double flowers.	
SIZE: 2½–5' or more tall.	
BLOOM TIME: Repeat-bloomers.	
FRAGRANCE: Many are fragrant.	
ZONES: 3–10.	

>Flower colors include all the usual shades.

>Plants are disease resistant and require minimal care.

SHRUB is a generic classification given to a diverse group of roses that don't fit neatly into any other category. Shrub roses vary from tidy bushes with small clusters of flowers to tall, arching plants or sprawling bushes ideal for hedges.

Outstanding traits of this group of roses are vigor, repeat bloom cycles, disease resistance, and low maintenance. These characteristics make shrub roses ideal plants for the landscape. They stand up to rigorous growing conditions and regularly reveal new flowers.

Some of the hardiest shrub roses include Griffith Buck roses, such as 'Carefree Beauty'; Canadian hybrids, such as the Morden Series, Explorer Series, and Parkland Series; and Meidiland roses, bred in France by the House of Meilland.

The beloved David Austin English roses are also members of the shrub roses group. They were created by crossing old garden roses with modern repeat-bloomers. Their petal-packed flowers and lush fragrance make them very popular.

< 56 >

Care: Low-maintenance strategies

These simple chores will ensure shrub roses are healthy and happy—and keep regular maintenance to a minimum.

ENCIRCLE PLANTS WITH MULCH. Spread a 2- to 3-inch layer of loose mulch, such as shredded bark or cocoa-bean hulls around, but not touching, the base of roses. Mulch will suppress weeds and conserve moisture.

USE A DRIP HOSE AND A TIMER to effortlessly and efficiently provide roses with 1 to 2 inches of water per week.

FEED WITH A SLOW-RELEASE PLANT FOOD. The simplest way to feed shrub roses is to use a complete plant food, such as Miracle-Gro Shake 'n Feed Continuous Release Rose Plant Food or Ortho Rose Pride Total Flower & Rose Care. These products are slow-release granules that feed roses and flowers for six weeks to three months in one easy step. Simply apply the granules around the base of the plant, mix into the top inch or two of soil, and water thoroughly. Repeat the process as directed on the package.

PRUNE ANNUALLY IN SPRING. Often a single spring pruning is all that is needed to keep shrub roses healthy and to maintain their form. Prune away dead and damaged canes in early spring. ❶ If shrub roses become overgrown or outgrow their boundaries, treat them like other shrubs in your yard. ❷ Use thinning cuts to open up the shrub, cutting stems back to a main branch and ❸ remove the oldest canes to make room for new growth.

Notes

_____
_____
_____
_____
_____

< 57 >

'DAYDREAM'

'HERITAGE'

'CAREFREE BEAUTY'

'KNOCK OUT'

SHRUB ROSES offer a multitude of colorful landscape solutions. Call on them to create low-maintenance hedges, mounding spots of color, and flower-rich ground covers.

'Carefree Beauty'

HARDY TO ZONE 4 • PINK FLOWERS • SIZE: 6 FEET TALL BY 5 FEET WIDE • LIGHT SCENT • GOOD DISEASE RESISTANCE • ARS RATING: 8.7

'Carefree Beauty' was bred to withstand the freezing winters of the upper Midwest. Its fragrant flowers are pink and open flat with a few irregular, loose petals at the center. They bloom singly or in clusters. 'Carefree Beauty' repeats flowering so that it is almost always in bloom during the growing season. This sprawling shrub is rarely plagued by pests. It was developed by Griffith Buck at Iowa State University.

< 58 >

'DayDream'

HARDY TO ZONE 4 • PINK FLOWERS • SIZE: 2 FEET TALL AND WIDE • LIGHT SCENT • EXCELLENT DISEASE RESISTANCE • AARS WINNER

Massive clusters of fuchsia-pink blooms cover 'DayDream' all summer long. Each lightly scented single blossom is wide and flat, resembling a little button. The plant's foliage is glossy, deep green and highly disease resistant. Its diminutive size and neat round habit make 'DayDream' a great plant for use as edging, in perennial flower borders, and at the front of shrub borders.

'Graham Thomas'

HARDY TO ZONE 5 • YELLOW FLOWERS • SIZE: 6 TO 8 FEET TALL BY 5 FEET WIDE • INTENSE SCENT • MODERATE DISEASE RESISTANCE • ARS RATING: 8.2

The flowers of 'Graham Thomas' are rich, bright, golden yellow, fading to lemon, especially in hot sunshine. The blooms are sometimes borne singly, but usually in long-stemmed clusters of three to nine. Some rose experts claim 'Graham Thomas' is the biggest and best yellow rose developed by David Austin. In hot climates, it gains height and flowers almost continuously when fed and watered regularly.

'Heritage'

HARDY TO ZONE 5 • PINK FLOWERS • SIZE: 4 FEET TALL AND 3 FEET WIDE • INTENSE SCENT • GOOD DISEASE RESISTANCE • ARS RATING: 8.4

The most popular of the David Austin English roses, 'Heritage' is very floriferous, boasting two or three full flushes of blooms each year with many lovely flowers in between. The flowers are pale salmon-pink at the center and cream or white toward the outside. The long, lax stems are almost thornless and will develop into stout canes, forming an upright shrub in a few years. This nearly pest-free plant grows best in cool climates.

'Knock Out'

HARDY TO ZONE 4 • RED FLOWERS • SIZE: 3 FEET TALL BY 4 FEET WIDE • MODERATE SCENT • EXCELLENT DISEASE RESISTANCE • AARS WINNER • ARS RATING: 8.4

Drought-tolerant, disease-free, and very hardy, 'Knock Out' is a wonderful example of a low-maintenance rose. Its cheerful light cherry colored flowers seem to glow with color. The abundant flowers are clustered in groups and adorn the plant daily from summer to fall. 'Blushing Knock Out', a light pink cultivar, has similar traits.

< 59 >

'MORDEN CENTENNIAL'

'NEARLY WILD'

'MARTHA'S VINEYARD'

'SALLY HOLMES'

'Martha's Vineyard'

HARDY TO ZONE 5 • PINK FLOWERS • SIZE: 3 FEET TALL AND 5 FEET WIDE • MINIMAL SCENT • GOOD DISEASE RESISTANCE • ARS RATING: 8.3

Hot-pink, semidouble flowers decorate this tall, vigorous plant. It is one of the later roses to begin flowering, but once it starts, there is no stopping it—massive clusters of flowers open one after another until fall. The canes are covered with little bristles, making this rose a good choice for an impenetrable hedge. The plant tolerates extreme heat and cold well and is disease resistant.

< 60 >

'Morden Centennial'

HARDY TO ZONE 3 • PINK FLOWERS • SIZE: 3 TO 5 FEET TALL AND WIDE • LIGHT SCENT • GOOD DISEASE RESISTANCE • ARS RATING: 8.4

A member of the Morden group of roses from the Canadian research station in Manitoba, 'Morden Centennial' is one of the most floriferous and cold-hardy shrub roses. Its flowers, borne singly or in clusters, are pale crimson at first but fade to bright pink as they open. Long-lasting bright red hips follow. 'Morden Centennial' has a large flush of flowers in early summer, small flushes throughout summer, and another big flush of flowers in fall. Deadheading improves fall flowering. The plant's dark, shiny leaves are generally healthy.

'Nearly Wild'

HARDY TO ZONES 4 • PINK FLOWERS • SIZE: 2 TO 3 FEET TALL AND 4 FEET WIDE • LIGHT SCENT • EXCELLENT DISEASE RESISTANCE • ARS RATING: 7.7

True to its name, 'Nearly Wild' does resemble a wild rose with its clusters of single pink and white flowers. It blooms constantly from early summer until fall. This low-growing plant forms an excellent low shrub; it is disease resistant.

'Sally Holmes'

HARDY TO ZONE 5 • WHITE FLOWERS • SIZE: 5 FEET TALL BY 6 FEET WIDE • LIGHT SCENT • MODERATE DISEASE RESISTANCE • ARS RATING: 8.9

Large clouds of snowy white blooms are the hallmark of 'Sally Holmes'. This large shrub rose thrives in hot climates where it will easily grow to 6 feet wide. Because of its dense, billowing habit, it may need staking. The plant flowers repeatedly throughout the season and is relatively pest-free, except for an occasional bout with black spot.

More great shrub roses

'FLOWER CARPET' (pink)
'MAGIC MEIDILAND' (dark pink)
'MORDEN BLUSH' (pink)
'PRAIRIE HARVEST' (butter-yellow)
'WINCHESTER CATHEDRAL' (white)

Notes

< 61 >

'THE APOTHECARY'S ROSE'

OLD GARDEN AND SPECIES ROSE BASICS

OVERALL FORM: Vigorous small to large shrubs; some climb or ramble.

SIZE: 3–15' tall and wide.

BLOOM TIME: Summer, some repeat in fall.

FRAGRANCE: Many have heady fragrance that varies from fruity to spicy.

ZONES: 4–10.

> The species vary in cold hardiness and disease resistance.

> Flower colors include white, pink, mauve, red, purple, and yellow; some have bicolored flowers.

OLD GARDEN ROSES—call them what you will: heirloom, antique, heritage, or old garden roses—and species (wild) roses are venerable beauties that never lose their charm. Coming to us through centuries of wild and cultivated growth, these easy-to-grow plants are survivors. They are disease resistant, need little care, and tolerate extreme climates. The exquisite beauty of their softly colored flowers parallels their famous, robust fragrance. Although they have a short vase-life, bouquets of old garden roses will perfume an entire room.

Most old garden and species roses bloom once a year, but some reveal flushes of flowers off and on from summer into fall. As shrubs, old garden and species roses reach various sizes, making attractive hedge or specimen plants. Choose from climbers, ramblers, and ground cover varieties.

< 62 >

Care: Taming old garden and species roses

Vigorous growers, some old garden roses and many species roses will send out long canes and in a few years take over a shrub or perennial border. This fearless growth makes them an excellent choice for a hedge or other large planting, but it can be challenging in a confined area. Keep newly planted old garden or species roses in check or tame an established plant with these tips.

❶ PRUNE WITH GUSTO. Most old garden and species roses take kindly to pruning, so regularly trim away wayward canes each spring. For extremely vigorous growers, a midsummer pruning might also be necessary to lessen the chore the following spring.

❷ REMOVE OLD CANES YEARLY. Cut back about one-half of the plant's oldest canes to the ground each year. The plant will shoot up new growth to compensate for the loss.

❸ RECLAIM OVERGROWN PLANTS.
Rejuvenate an overgrown rose bush over a three-year period. In the first year, remove one-third of the oldest canes and all weak, damaged, and thin shoots. In year two, remove half of the remaining old stems, and in the third year, cut back all remaining woody stems.

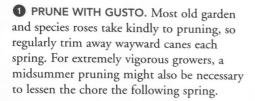

Notes

_____
_____
_____
_____
_____
_____
_____
_____

< **63** >

'CÉLINE FORESTIER'

'CELSIANA'

'THE APOTHECARY'S ROSE'

'CHARLES DE MILLS'

OLD GARDEN AND SPECIES ROSES are at home everywhere from the cottage garden to a shrub border. Plant these fragrant bloomers where you can enjoy their perfume, or harvest bouquets for enjoying indoors.

'The Apothecary's Rose' *(Rosa gallica officinalis)*
HARDY TO ZONE 4 • PINK FLOWERS • SIZE: 3 TO 4 FEET TALL AND WIDE • INTENSE SCENT • GOOD DISEASE RESISTANCE • ARS RATING: 8.6

First cultivated prior to 1600, 'The Apothecary's Rose' has an intense fragrance. The semidouble flowers have a cushion of golden stamens in the center. Surrounding petals change from bright crimson to purple. Harvest and dry the flower petals for potpourri. Fall brings lovely dark green foliage and attractive rose hips.

< 64 >

'Céline Forestier'

HARDY TO ZONE 7 • PALE YELLOW FLOWERS • SIZE: 13 FEET TALL BY 6½ FEET WIDE • INTENSE SCENT • GOOD DISEASE RESISTANCE • ARS RATING: 8.8

In summer, pillows of pale yellow petals form flowers in clusters of three to five blooms on 'Céline Forestier'. Hints of buff, apricot, or pink often decorate the fully double flowers, which have an intense spicy fragrance. Tolerant of poor soils and hot climates, this rose is an excellent choice for Southern gardens.

'Celsiana'

HARDY TO ZONE 5 • PINK FLOWERS SIZE: 6½ FEET TALL BY 5 FEET WIDE • INTENSE SCENT • GOOD DISEASE RESISTANCE • ARS RATING: 8.8

One of the longest flowering of the once-flowering roses, 'Celsiana' has clusters of five to seven flowers with rose-pink petals that quickly fade to very pale pink. The crinkled, delicate flowers exude a wonderfully rich fragrance. The plant is tall and strong, with a lot of small prickles and gray-green leaves. 'Celsiana' makes a good impenetrable hedge. It benefits from a light pruning immediately after flowering.

'Charles de Mills'

HARDY TO ZONE 5 • RED FLOWERS • SIZE: 4 TO 6 FEET TALL AND WIDE • LIGHT SCENT • MODERATE DISEASE RESISTANCE • ARS RATING: 8.4

The flowers of this romantic favorite range from dark red to crimson to rich purple. They can reach up to 5 inches wide and have a light, sweet fragrance. The flowers hold their petals well on the bush and also make good cutting flowers. The almost-thornless plant has green, rugged leaves and a naturally arching habit. Because it is susceptible to mildew, provide at least 2 feet of space around plants for air circulation.

'Hansa' (Rosa rugosa)

HARDY TO ZONE 4 • DARK PINK FLOWERS • SIZE: 6 FEET TALL BY 5 FEET WIDE • INTENSE SCENT • EXCELLENT DISEASE RESISTANCE • ARS RATING: 8.4

One of the best rugosa roses, 'Hansa' is very easy to grow and flowers sporadically all summer. Its long and elegant buds open into semidouble masses of silky magenta petals around a thick cluster of golden stamens. Large vermilion hips follow the intensely fragrant flowers if not deadheaded. 'Hansa' has very thorny canes. This energetic and disease-free rose will spread and is good for hedging.

'HANSA'

'HARISON'S YELLOW'

'QUEEN OF DENMARK'   'ROSA MUNDI'

'Harison's Yellow'

**HARDY TO ZONE 4 • YELLOW FLOWERS • SIZE: 6 FEET TALL AND WIDE •
MODERATE SCENT • MODERATE DISEASE RESISTANCE • ARS RATING: 8.2**
An exceptionally adaptable rose, 'Harison's Yellow' thrives in poor or rich
soil, dry or wet climates, and hot or cold areas. Its clear yellow flowers
appear in early summer and are small and have a fruity scent. It grows as
a dense shrub for the first few years, but later sends up long, open,
arching stems.

< 66 >

'Mme. Hardy'

HARDY TO ZONE 5 • WHITE FLOWERS • SIZE: 6 FEET TALL AND 5 FEET WIDE • MODERATE SCENT • GOOD DISEASE RESISTANCE • ARS RATING: 9.0

'Mme. Hardy' sums up all that is most beautiful and desirable in old roses. The form of the flowers is exquisite, and their light scent is delicious. Although the purest of all white roses when fully open, there is a hint of pink in the bud. 'Mme. Hardy' only blooms once in spring, but the show is spectacular. The healthy green foliage forms a wonderful backdrop in the garden throughout the growing season.

'Queen of Denmark' (also called 'Königin von Dänemark')

HARDY TO ZONE 4 • PINK FLOWERS • SIZE: 5 FEET TALL AND 3 FEET WIDE • INTENSE SCENT • GOOD DISEASE RESISTANCE • ARS RATING: 8.6

This old rose's petal-packed, cotton-candy-pink flowers bloom in large clusters, often pulling the canes to the ground in an arch. The large flat flowers are 3 to 4 inches wide and strongly fragrant. The compact plant blooms once in late spring or early summer and has thorny canes. Use 'Queen of Denmark' as an informal hedge.

'Rosa Mundi'

HARDY TO ZONE 5 • PINK AND WHITE STRIPED FLOWERS • SIZE: 4 FEET TALL AND 3 FEET WIDE • INTENSE SCENT • GOOD DISEASE RESISTANCE

Also known as 'Versicolor', 'Rosa Mundi' is the oldest striped rose known. Its blooms are semidouble, usually 4 inches wide, with red and pink stripes against a white background accented by golden-yellow stamens. No two petals are alike on this intensely fragrant rose. This once-blooming plant has a sprawling habit. It is a good hedge plant. More great old garden and species roses

'BARONNE PRÉVOST' (rose pink)
'JACQUES CARTIER' (light pink)
'ROSA GLAUCA' (lilac-pink flowers and grayish-purple foliage)
'SOMBREUIL' (white)
'STANWELL PERPETUAL' (blush pink)

Notes

_____
_____
_____
_____
_____

< 67 >

'MUTABILIS'

'Mutabilis'

HARDY TO ZONE 7 • ORANGE AND PINK FLOWERS • SIZE: 6 FEET TALL AND 8 FEET WIDE • LIGHT SCENT • GOOD DISEASE RESISTANCE • ARS RATING: 8.9

Widely grown and popular in warm regions, this rose is never without flowers. The lightly fragrant flowers open orange or buff-yellow before turning to pink and ending in pale crimson. Long, slender crimson stems carry the flowers in small clusters. 'Mutabilis' has large prickles and climbs with training, but it looks best as a shrub.

< 68 >

'BALLERINA'

'CAREFREE WONDER'

'THE PRINCE'

SOME ROSES GROW IN SHADE

To grow most roses successfully, all-day sunshine is a must. Yet even if your garden receives sun for only four hours a day, there are a few roses that you can grow with ease. These shade-friendly roses commonly have just a single or double layer of petals surrounding the center of the flower and glossy leaves that resist mildew and black spot that shaded sites promote. Keep in mind that these roses need sufficient heat for the petals to open naturally.

Although most petal-packed flowers may never open properly in low-light conditions, there are a few exceptions. Here are several recommendations for those who wish to grow full-petaled roses in shady conditions.

< 70 >

'Ballerina'
4 FEET TALL AND WIDE; FLORIBUNDA; HARDY TO ZONE 4.
A graceful, rounded plant, 'Ballerina' blooms profusely with large clusters of medium pink flowers.

'Buff Beauty'
4 TO 5 FEET TALL AND WIDE; OLD GARDEN ROSE; HARDY TO ZONE 5.
Clusters of apricot-yellow flowers on arching canes highlight 'Buff Beauty'.

'Carefree Wonder'
3 TO 4 FEET TALL AND WIDE; SHRUB ROSE; HARDY TO ZONE 4.
Bright pink blooms cover 'Carefree Wonder' from spring until frost. This hardy, disease-resistant, low-maintenance shrub is invaluable in the landscape.

'Cornelia'
6 TO 8 FEET LONG; HYBRID TEA; HARDY TO ZONE 4.
A sweet fragrance accompanies the salmon-pink flowers that cover the arching canes of 'Cornelia' for several weeks in early summer.

'Ice Meidiland'
1½ FEET TALL AND 6 FEET WIDE; SHRUB ROSE; HARDY TO ZONE 4.
The clear white flowers of 'Ice Meidiland' glow in partly shaded sites. This low-growing plant is low maintenance and disease resistant. '

'The Prince'
2 TO 3 FEET TALL; SHRUB ROSE; HARDY TO ZONE 4.
'The Prince' has 4-inch-wide, deep crimson, fragrant flowers.

SHADY SUCCESS
Grow great shade-friendly roses with these planting and care tips.

- ENCOURAGE MORE LIGHT where possible. If trees are casting shadows on your roses, selectively prune the trees to allow light to filter through the canopy. Hire an arborist to thin the branches while maintaining a structurally sound tree.

- AIM FOR AFTERNOON SHADE rather than morning shade. When possible, plant roses where they will receive morning light. Morning sunlight quickly dries leaves and reduces disease trouble.

- GOOD AIR CIRCULATION is a must. Another tool for fighting disease, good air circulation helps dry leaves and discourage disease. Avoid planting roses near dense hedges and evergreens, which will limit air movement.

'BERRIES 'N CREAM'

'DUBLIN BAY'

'CLIMBING CECILE BRÜNNER'   'SOMBREUIL'

Surround yourself with flowers by growing climbing roses on an arch, arbor, or pergola. Each of these freestanding structures adds vertical interest to your garden. Even the smallest area can accommodate an arch, but arbors, which are essentially large arches, and pergolas, which are used to create outdoor rooms, need more space. Whatever the support you choose, it must be strong, because it has to support the substantial weight of the flowering canes.

The best roses to grow on these structures flower from ground level to the tips of their long canes. They bloom equally well on vertical and horizontal planes and produce canes at least 12 to 15 feet long, so that two plants can overlap and intertwine at the midpoint of the arch or pergola. Choose a self-cleaning rose that doesn't require constant grooming. Look for fragrant climbers to heighten your pleasure.

< 72 >

'Aloha'

10 TO 12 FEET; CLIMBING HYBRID TEA; HARDY TO ZONE 5.

Elegant, hybrid tealike deep-pink flowers decorate 'Aloha'. This rose is a slow grower; it tolerates poor soils with ease.

'Berries 'n Cream'

10 TO 20 FEET; LARGE-FLOWERED CLIMBER; HARDY TO ZONE 5.

The strong stems of 'Berries 'n Cream' bear flowers swirled with old-rose pink and creamy white in bouquetlike clusters.

'Climbing Cécile Brünner'

20 FEET LONG; CLIMBING POLYANTHA; HARDY TO ZONE 6.

Almost always in flower, 'Climbing Cécile Brünner' has large clusters of silvery pink blooms with a spicy, sweet fragrance.

'Dublin Bay'

10 TO 12 FEET; LARGE-FLOWERED CLIMBER; HARDY TO ZONE 4.

The rich red flowers of 'Dublin Bay' are velvety and sumptuous and, on established plants, appear throughout the summer. 'Dublin Bay' is slow to establish in the first season, but once it takes off in the second season it is a very reliable plant.

'Sombreuil'

6 TO 12 FEET; CLIMBING TEA; HARDY TO ZONE 7.

This old garden rose has masses of fragrant, creamy-white flowers that cover the plant for weeks during the growing season.

'Zéphirine Drouhin'

10 TO 12 FEET; CLIMBING OLD GARDEN ROSE; HARDY TO ZONE 5.

Rose-pink, sweetly scented flowers blanket thornless 'Zéphirine Drouhin' from early summer until frost.

UPWARD BOUND

Climbing roses do not naturally climb. If left alone, they tend to mound and sprawl. Train roses to reach lofty heights with these tips.

- BEGIN TRAINING A CLIMBING ROSE shortly after planting. As soon as the canes can reach a support, use twine or raffia to secure them to the structure.

- AS THE CANES GROW, continue tying them to the support every 12 inches.

- PRUNE CLIMBING ROSES as needed in early spring and after flowering to keep wayward canes in check.

'BETTY BOOP'

'BONICA'

'CHINA DOLL' HEDGE

'KNOCK OUT'

Thanks to their thicketlike character, roses are an excellent choice when you want to create privacy screens, block out ugly views, or divide the garden into rooms—and offer more color and interest than a formal hedge. Plus, their thorny canes create impenetrable barriers that are useful for keeping some pests out of the garden.

Rose hedges vary in height but tend to be between 3 and 6 feet tall. Retain the shrubs' natural bushy form, but plant them close enough to create a unified look. Space shrub roses and floribundas, which mature to 3 to 4 feet wide, about 2 feet apart for a dense hedge. Climbers, planted farther apart, give a similar but looser look.

< 74 >

'Betty Boop'

3 TO 5 FEET TALL; FLORIBUNDA; HARDY TO ZONE 5.

The eye-catching red and white blooms of this floribunda have a fruity fragrance. 'Betty Boop' is a reliable plant and reblooms well.

'Bonica'

3 TO 5 FEET TALL; SHRUB ROSE; HARDY TO ZONE 4.

Apple-scented, round pink flowers fill the arching canes of 'Bonica' for several weeks in summer. As fall approaches, attractive bright-orange hips replace the flowers.

'Carefree Sunshine'

3 TO 4 FEET TALL; SHRUB ROSE; HARDY TO ZONE 4.

This lovely golden-yellow rose thrives in hot summers and has blooms that won't fade in the heat.

'Knock Out'

3 TO 4 FEET TALL; SHRUB ROSE; HARDY TO ZONE 4.

Raspberry-red flowers cover this easy-to-grow shrub rose from early summer until fall. Disease free.

'Nearly Wild'

2 TO 3 FEET TALL; FLORIBUNDA; HARDY TO ZONE 4.

A good choice for a short hedge, 'Nearly Wild' has fragrant single pink blooms.

'Starry Night'

3 TO 5 FEET TALL; SHRUB ROSE; HARDY TO ZONE 5.

Single white flowers illuminate 'Starry Night' throughout the growing season. The plant's glossy foliage has excellent disease resistance.

REJUVENATE YOUR HEDGE

Keep your rose hedge vigorous and healthy by rejuvenating it every three years or so. Rejuvenation is a process of removing one-third to one-half of the old, thick canes to promote the growth of new shoots. If left to grow, these large woody shoots will stifle new growth and the hedge will eventually become lean and lanky.

To rejuvenate a rose hedge, prune back one-third to one-half of the old canes to ground level in spring. The following year remove one-third of the remaining old canes and in the third year remove the last of the old, thick canes. Begin the process again in two to three years.

'GERTRUDE JEKYLL'

'INTRIGUE'

'THE FAIRY'

'SUN FLARE', 'LAVENDER CREAM' AND 'TRUMPETER' ROSES WITH PERENNIALS

Mixed borders bring together trees, shrubs, bulbs, annuals, and perennials to create colorful, long-lasting landscape beauty. A mixed border might accent a hedge, wall, or fence, or it might be freestanding in the lawn and act as a barrier between two separate areas.

Roses fit well in mixed borders, especially those with long blooming seasons. Upright varieties are useful where you want to create a tightly woven tapestry of colors, yet the rounded profiles of once-blooming shrub roses work well too. Even when not blooming, they add calm spots between areas of color.

In borders, the tallest plants often stand at the back, the shorter ones in the front. But a well-placed rose can create the perfect accent—in front or mid-border—where its form and blooms can stand out.

< 76 >

'Astrid Lindgren'
3 TO 4 FEET TALL; SHRUB ROSE; HARDY TO ZONE 4.
A dense, compact bush, 'Astrid Lindgren' is adorned with clusters of double pink flowers throughout the season. The flowers are excellent for cutting.

'Gertrude Jekyll'
5 TO 6 FEET; SHRUB ROSE; HARDY TO ZONE 5.
Glowing pink blossoms make 'Gertrude Jekyll' one of David Austin's most popular roses. The vigorous rose looks best if kept to a height of 2 to 3 feet in a mixed border. Deadheading is essential for this rose to rebloom.

'Intrigue'
3 TO 4 FEET TALL; FLORIBUNDA; HARDY TO ZONE 5.
An attention grabber, 'Intrigue' has rich purple flowers with many petals. This repeat bloomer is fragrant.

'Pat Austin'
4 TO 5 FEET TALL; SHRUB ROSE; HARDY TO ZONE 6.
The copper-coral flowers of this David Austin rose have a strong, fruity scent.

'Peter Mayle'
4 TO 6 FEET TALL; SHRUB ROSE; HARDY TO ZONE 5.
A good choice for the back of the border, lofty 'Peter Mayle' has huge red, hybrid-tealike flowers on straight stems.

'The Fairy'
2 TO 3 FEET TALL; POLYANTHA; HARDY TO ZONE 4.
Almost always in bloom, 'The Fairy' is blanketed with apple-scented blossoms. This low-growing plant is good for the front of the border.

COLOR IN THE GARDEN
A mixed border is often made up of a mix of colors as well as a mix of plants. With a rainbow of hues at your fingertips, selecting colors for a border is a daunting task. Mix and match colors and experiment with color combinations until you find a group of colors that you like. Keep these tips in mind as you "paint" your border.

- A COOL COLOR PALETTE will make a small garden feel larger. Pink, lemon-yellow, lavender, and blue visually expand a space and have a calming effect.

- WARM, INTENSE COLORS are attention grabbers and look wonderful in sunny spots at midday.

- USE YELLOW, WHITE, AND PASTELS in gardens that will be enjoyed primarily at dusk. These colors capture the light and glow as the sun goes down.

'FRAGRANT CLOUD'

'CHRYSLER IMPERIAL'

'CONSTANCE SPRY'

'SHIELA'S PERFUME'

The legendary perfume of roses is often reason enough to grow the enduring beauties. The scent of roses is determined by their genes and varies from faint to elusive to heady and intoxicating. As complex as any perfume, rose fragrance echoes apple, citrus, honey, myrrh, musk, and raspberry, evoking descriptions such as sweet, spicy, and fruity.

Old garden roses are often masterpieces of fragrance. New breeding trends emphasize scent, although many modern rose breeders still concentrate on achieving ideal form, color, and habit at the expense of fragrance. If you have questions about a rose's fragrance before purchasing a plant, learn more about the rose and its scent in a reliable rose encyclopedia before making a purchase.

< 78 >

'Chrysler Imperial'
4 TO 6 FEET TALL; HYBRID TEA; HARDY TO ZONE 6.
This popular hybrid tea has a strong, rich scent and a multitude of crimson flowers. It grows best in cool weather.

'Constance Spry'
4 TO 8 FEET TALL; SHRUB ROSE; HARDY TO ZONE 4.
Soft pink flowers of 'Constance Spry' exude a delightful myrrh fragrance. This vigorous plant is often grown as a climber or against a wall.

'Fragrant Cloud'
3 TO 5 FEET TALL; HYBRID TEA; HARDY TO ZONE 4.
Large coral flowers with a rich, fruity fragrance decorate 'Fragrant Cloud' for weeks.

'Henry Hudson'
3 TO 4 FEET TALL; HYBRID RUGOSA; HARDY TO ZONE 4.
Double white flowers with a hint of pink adorn 'Henry Hudson' from early summer until frost. The flowers have a strong, sweet fragrance.

'Iceberg'
3 TO 4 FEET TALL; FLORIBUNDA; HARDY TO ZONE 5.
Small clusters of fragrant double blooms decorate this easy-to-grow rose.

'Sheila's Perfume'
3 TO 4 FEET TALL; FLORIBUNDA; HARDY TO ZONE 5.
The elegant yellow and deep-pink flowers of 'Sheila's Perfume' have an intense rose-and-fruit scent.

PERFUME YOUR WORLD
Ensure that you actually do take time to stop and smell the roses with these tips on where to plant fragrant bloomers in the landscape.

- NEAR A DOOR OR WINDOW. Provided there is at least six hours of direct sunlight, plant fragrant roses near a door or window that can be opened so the lovely fragrance can drift inside.

- ALONGSIDE A BENCH OR SEATING AREA. Perfume a garden seating area with a fragrant rose. Add an arbor over a bench for shade and plant a fragrant climbing rose to scramble up the structure to provide additional shade and wonderful scent.

- BESIDE A PATIO OR DECK. Plant fragrant roses near your patio or deck and take in the sweet scent as you enjoy the outdoor space.

THE BEST ROSES FOR CUT FLOWERS

'KARDINAL'

'LOVE & PEACE'

CUTTING ROSES   'SEXY REXY'

Bring the beauty of roses indoors with a cut-flower bouquet. Fragrant and colorful rose bouquets, no matter how small, make eye-catching, sweetly scented additions to your desktop, nightstand, or kitchen table. Several types of roses make excellent cut flowers.

Hybrid teas can't be beat for cut flowers, although they are sometimes leggy, unattractive plants in the garden. Their long, sturdy stems, elegant buds, and long-lasting blooms make them perfect for bouquets and flower arranging. When choosing hybrid teas look for many-petaled flowers, which take longer to open than blooms with fewer petals and thus last longer in the vase.

Grandifloras and floribundas also make good cut flowers. Both bear clusters of flowers on long canes that are instant bouquets-on-a-stem. When selecting grandifloras and floribundas for a bouquet, look for stems that contain a mix of open flowers, flowers still in bud, and partially open flowers.

Old garden roses also make glorious arrangements. Their fragrance can be nearly overwhelming, a powerful, sweet scent that wafts through several

< 80 >

rooms of the house. Full old-rose blossoms with many petals rest heavily on their stems and droop gracefully over the edge of a vase. Unlike long-stemmed hybrid teas, old-rose stems are short and flexible and often bear small sprays of flowers. Extend the life of your cut-flower bouquet with the tips on page 37.

'Céline Forestier'
5 TO 6 FEET TALL; OLD GARDEN ROSE; HARDY TO ZONE 7.

The large old garden rose has fully double, fragrant, creamy white flowers. A repeat bloomer, 'Céline Forestier' is a vigorous plant with healthy foliage.

'Kardinal'
4 TO 6 FEET TALL; HYBRID TEA; HARDY TO ZONE 5.

Classic red roses top the long stems of 'Kardinal', a hybrid tea. The lightly fragrant flowers last for several days after cutting.

'Love & Peace'
5 TO 6 FEET TALL; HYBRID TEA; HARDY TO ZONE 5.

Prized for its striking yellow and deep-pink flower, 'Love & Peace' blooms best in humid climates.

'Royal Highness'
5 TO 7 FEET TALL; HYBRID TEA; HARDY TO ZONE 5.

Large, pale-pink blooms adorn 'Royal Highness', a hybrid tea rose. Borne singly on long straight stems, the blooms have a sweet tea fragrance and open slowly. Plants are vigorous and exceptionally disease-resistant.

'Sexy Rexy'
4 TO 5 FEET TALL; FLORIBUNDA; HARDY TO ZONE 5.

The upright stems of 'Sexy Rexy', a floribunda, support clusters of 20 or more pink blooms that resemble camellias when fully opened. Deadhead spent flowers to encourage rebloom.

'Showbiz'
3 TO 4 FEET TALL; FLORIBUNDA; HARDY TO ZONE 5.

Great clusters of fire-engine red blooms decorate easy-to-grow 'Showbiz', a floribunda. It has excellent disease resistance.

'Sombreuil'
6 TO 12 FEET TALL; CLIMBING TEA; HARDY TO ZONE 7.

Fragrant, double flowers decorate 'Sombreuil', an old garden rose, as it climbs or sprawls onto nearby structures. Cut blooms when they are partially open for best results.

< 81 >

'FRENCH LACE'

'KNOCK OUT'

A POTTED ROSE STANDARD

'MINNIE PEARL'

Roses grown in containers bring season-long color and fragrance to decks, patios, and balconies. Potted roses also work well as focal points in formal gardens and as border accents. Though many roses grow well in containers, the best choices are those that stay narrow and upright or form dense floral mounds.

Containers made of terra-cotta, wood, or plastic work well for growing roses. Whatever container you choose will work if it has the right shape and size. For miniatures use a 5- to 7-gallon container that's wider than it is deep. For floribundas, choose a 10- to 12-gallon size. For hybrid teas and large shrubs, use a 20-gallon tub, urn, or box.

< 82 >

'French Lace'
3 TO 4 FEET TALL; FLORIBUNDA; HARDY TO ZONE 6.
Best suited for a 15-gallon or larger container, 'French Lace', a floribunda, has clusters of creamy-white flowers with a mild, fruity fragrance.

'Hot Tamale'
1 FOOT TALL; MINIATURE ROSE; HARDY TO ZONE 5.
A nonstop show of yellow-orange blooms color 'Hot Tamale', a miniature rose.

'Ingrid Bergman'
5 TO 6 FEET TALL; HYBRID TEA; HARDY TO ZONE 5.
Powerfully fragrant, velvety red flowers decorate 'Ingrid Bergman' throughout the summer. The flowers are excellent for cutting.

'Knock Out'
3 TO 5 FEET TALL; SHRUB ROSE; HARDY TO ZONE 4.
Completely disease-free, 'Knock Out' is loaded with light-red or deep-pink flowers in large clusters.

'Minnie Pearl'
1 TO 2 FEET TALL; MINIATURE ROSE; HARDY TO ZONE 5.
This miniature rose has elegant buds that open to lovely, light pink flowers. 'Minnie Pearl' repeat blooms several times during summer and early fall.

'Party Girl'
1 TO 2 FEET TALL; MINIATURE ROSE; HARDY TO ZONE 5.
Large clusters of apricot-yellow blooms adorn 'Party Girl', a miniature rose.

GROWING ROSES IN CONTAINERS

- The proper soil in a container ensures blooming success. First, put a 2-inch layer of peat moss in the bottom of the container. Add a premium potting-soil mix around the plant's roots or root ball, stopping when the soil is 2 inches from the lip of the pot.

- To preserve water during the hot summer months, top the pot with a 2-inch layer of bark mulch. Also, put a saucer under the container to catch excess water.

- Feed container roses regularly every two weeks; prevent build-up of salts by flushing the soil with water several times in succession every four weeks during dry weather.

- In Zones 1 through 7 do not leave plants or containers outside over winter. Bury them or bring them into a cool, frost-free location such as an attached garage or unheated basement.

ROSES AND LONG-BLOOMING COMPANIONS

Sweetly perfumed roses and long-blooming perennials happily mingle in this 12-foot-wide circular planting bed. Perfect for a small landscape, this planting bed is at home in the front or backyard and is especially striking when viewed from above.

The bed wakes up in midspring when the perennials and a few spring bulbs send up bright green leaves. The roses and perennials come into glorious bloom in mid-June, revealing flushed pastel, multipetal flowers for several weeks. After a brief siesta in the heat of summer, the roses and perennials stage a small second bloom at the end of August and into September. A bevy of chrysanthemums decorate the garden in fall.

Romantica roses, prized for their old-fashioned appearance, strong fragrance, and disease resistance, are planted throughout the garden. Vigorous plants, Romantica roses can easily grow 4 to 5 feet tall.

< 84 >

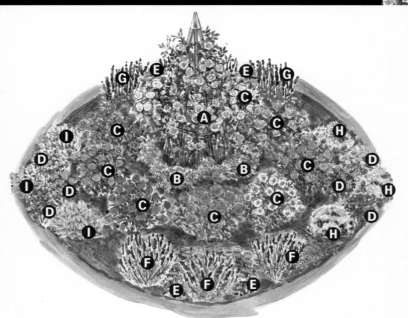

A ROSE-CLAD ARBOR AND WALKWAY

Roses grow alongside old-fashioned perennials, creating a visual feast in this walk-through garden. Perfect for transitioning from one garden to another or from the front yard to the backyard, this easy-care garden is a good choice for several areas in the landscape.

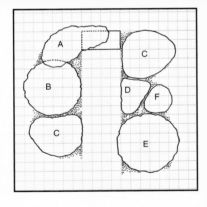

Climbing rose 'Carnea' scrambles up and over the vaulted arbor, an important element in achieving the look of a softer, older garden that flows from one area to another. Other good climbing roses include 'Cécile Brünner', 'Mermaid', Mme. Ernst Calvat', 'New Dawn', 'Sombreuil', and 'Zephirine Drouhin'. Foxgloves, pinks, hydrangeas, and verbena line the brick walkway.

< 86 >

PLANT LIST FOR AN AREA 18' × 17'

- **Ⓐ** 1 Species rose *(ROSA MULTIFLORA 'CARNEA')*: Zones 5–9
- **Ⓑ** 1 Shrub rose *(ROSA 'BALLERINA')*: Zones 5–9
- **Ⓒ** 12 Clump verbena *(VERBENA CANADENSIS)*: Zones 6–11
- **Ⓓ** 6 Pinks *(DIANTHUS SPP.)*: Zones 3–10, depending on species
- **Ⓔ** 1 'Hills of Snow' hydrangea *(HYDRANGEA ARBORESCENS 'HILLS OF SNOW')*: Zones 4–9
- **Ⓕ** 3 Common foxglove *(DIGITALIS PURPUREA)*: Zones 4–8

A ROSY HILLSIDE

Opulent roses, mounds of pink pincushion flowers, and soldier-straight foxgloves carry out a gentle color scheme in this hillside garden. The strong horizontal lines of the railroad ties anchoring the base of the slope are softened by cascades of white sweet alyssum

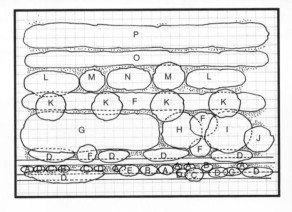

dancing alongside dainty purple lobelia and pink phlox.

Fragrant by day and luminous by night, this garden owes much of its allure to the interplay of perpendicular lines. Upright standard roses and tall foxgloves exaggerate the garden's upward sweep and contrast with the horizontal layers of color. Repetition creates a rhythmic sense of order, resulting in chords of color rather than a series of individual notes.

< 88 >

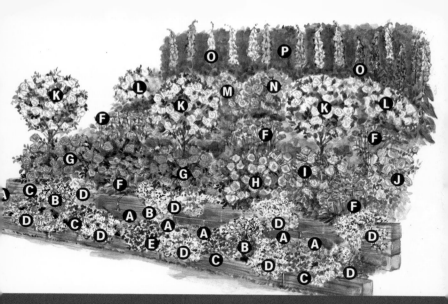

PLANT LIST FOR AN AREA 29' × 18'

- **Ⓐ** 6 Phlox *(PHLOX DRUMMONDII)*: Annual
- **Ⓑ** 3 Nicotiana *(NICOTIANA HYBRIDS)*: Annual
- **Ⓒ** 4 Viola *(VIOLA 'PENNY AZURE WING')*: Annual
- **Ⓓ** 20 Sweet alyssum *(LOBULARIA MARITIMA)*: Annual
- **Ⓔ** 1 Lobelia *(LOBELIA ERINUS)*: Annual
- **Ⓕ** 12 Pincushion flower *(SCABIOSA COLUMBARIA)*: Zones 3–9
- **Ⓖ** 4 **'GERTRUDE JEKYLL'** rose: Zones 5–9
- **Ⓗ** 1 **'HERITAGE'** rose: Zones 5–9
- **Ⓘ** 1 **'KATHERINE MORLEY'** rose : Zones 5–9
- **Ⓙ** 1 **'ABRAHAM DARBY'** rose: Zones 4–9
- **Ⓚ** 4 **'ICEBERG'** rose: Zones 6–9
- **Ⓛ** 2 **'MARGARET MERRIL'** rose: Zones 5–10
- **Ⓜ** 1 **'SHEER BLISS'** rose: Zones 6–10
- **Ⓝ** 1 **'HERO'** rose: Zones 4–9
- **Ⓞ** 20 Foxglove *(DIGITALIS PURPUREA)*: Zones 4–8
- **Ⓟ** 25 Rosemary *(ROSMARINUS OFFICINALIS)*: Zones 8–10

ROSES WITH THYME, LAMB'S-EARS, PENSTEMON, AND SHASTA DAISY

Combine your favorite roses with a bevy of annuals, perennials, bulbs, and shrubs for a healthy garden that has eye-catching interest year-round. Call on companion plants to cover up the lanky legs of your hybrid tea roses, provide a splash of color in early spring before roses wake up from their winter slumber, or add lacy or bold texture to a planting. Companion plants can also help deter pests. For example, alliums, such as garlic, onions, chives, and ornamental varieties, deter aphids and other pests.

When selecting companions for roses, choose plants that bloom in spring, summer, and fall to ensure that the garden is bursting with color from the time the garden comes alive in spring until frost.

< 90 >

Spring

COTTAGE PINK *(Dianthus plumarius):* Zones 3–8
DAFFODIL *(Narcissus* cultivars): Zones 3–8
GRAPE HYACINTH *(Muscari armeniacum):* Zones 4–8
IRIS *(Iris* species): Zones 3–9
PANSY *(Viola × wittrockiana* cultivars): Annual
PEONY *(Paeonia* hybrids): Zones 3–8
SNOWDROP *(Galanthus* species): Zones 4–9
TULIP *(Tulipa* cultivars): Zones 4–8

Summer

CATMINT *(Nepeta × faassenii):* Zones 3–8
CLEMATIS *(Clematis* cultivars): Zones 4–9
COLUMBINE *(Aquilegia* hybrids): Zones 3–9
CUSHION SPURGE *(Euphorbia polychroma):* Zones 4–9
DAYLILY *(Hemerocallis* cultivars): Zones 3–10
ENGLISH LAVENDER *(Lavandula angustifolia):* Zones 5–8
LADY'S MANTLE *(Alchemilla mollis):* Zones 4–7
LAMB'S-EARS *(Stachys byzantina):* Zones 4–8
LARKSPUR *(Consolida ambigua):* Annual
'MAY NIGHT' SALVIA *(Salvia sylvestris):* Zones 5–9
ORNAMENTAL ONION *(Allium* species): Zones 4–10
VERBENA *(Verbena bonariensis):* Annual
WORMWOOD *(Artemisia* species): Zones 4–9

Fall

CHRYSANTHEMUM *(Chrysanthemum* species): Zones 4–9
HYBRID ANEMONE *(Anemone hybrida):* Zones 4–8
NEW ENGLAND ASTER *(Aster novae-angliae):* Zones 4–8
STONECROP *(Sedum spectabile):* Zones 4–9

Notes

< 91 >

INDEX

A
'About Face', 38
'Abraham Darby', 89
All-America Rose
  Selection (AARS), 7
Alliums, 90
'Aloha', 73
'America', 54
American Rose Society
  (ARS), 7
Aphids, 30, 90
'The Apothecary's Rose',
  62, 64
Arbor and walkway plan,
  86–87
Arbors, 72–73
'Astrid Lindgren', 77

B
'Ballerina', 71, 87
Bare-root roses
  about, 6–7
  buying, 7
  fall and winter care,
    22–23
  planting, 10–11
  pruning, 10
  spring care, 18
  summer care, 21
Beetles, Japanese, 29
'Berries 'n' Cream', 73
'Betty Boop', 75
'Betty Prior', 42
'Black Jade', 50
Black spot, 26
'Blaze', 55
'Bonica', 75
Borders, mixed, 76–77
Bud union, 10
'Buff Beauty', 71

C
Canadian hybrid shrub
  roses, 56
Cane borers, 25
Canes, removing, 16, 17,
  63
Cankers, 25
'Carefree Beauty', 58
'Carefree Sunshine', 75
'Carefree Wonder', 71
'Carnea', 87
Catmint, 91
'Cécile Brünner', 46
'Céline Forestier', 65, 81
'Celsiana', 65
'Charisma', 40
'Charles de Mills', 65
'Cherry Parfait', 39

'China Doll', 47
Chrysanthemum, 85, 91
'Chrysler Imperial', 79
Clematis, 91
'Climbing Cécile
  Brünner', 73
Climbing roses, 52–55
  basic information, 52
  best choices for, 73,
    86
  cultivars, 54–55
  deadheading, 53
  in garden plan, 85
  pruning, 53, 73
  training, 18, 73
  winterizing, 22–23, 53
Columbine, 91
Common foxglove, 87
Companion plants,
  90–91
'Constance Spry', 79
Container-grown roses
  about, 6
  best choices for,
    82–83
  buying, 7
  containers for, 82
  fall and winter care,
    22–23
  growing tips, 83
  planting, 11
  spring care, 18
  summer care, 21
Containers, 49, 82
'Cornelia', 71
Cottage pink, 91
Cushion Spurge, 91

D
Daffodil, 91
David Austin English
  roses, 56
'DayDream', 59
Daylily, 91
Deadheading, 16, 21
'Dick Koster', 44
Disbudding flowers, 21
Diseases, 26–27
Drip irrigation system, 12
'Dublin Bay', 73

E
'Elle', 34
English Lavender, 91

F
'The Fairy', 77
Fall companion plants,
  91

Fall rose care, 22–23
Feeding
  granular plant food,
    14, 15
  schedule for, 14, 25
  springtime, 18
  summertime, 21
  water-soluble
    plant food, 14, 15
Fertilizing. See Feeding
Flood bubblers, 12
Floribundas, 40–43
  basic information, 40
  for bouquets, 80
  caring for, 41
  containers for, 82
  cultivars, 42–43
  for hedges, 41, 74
Flowers
  for bouquets, best
    roses for, 80–81
  for bouquets, cutting,
    21
  deadheading, 16, 21
  disbudding, 21
  pinching, 21
Flower thrips, 28
Foxglove, 87, 89
'Fragrant Cloud', 79
Fragrant rose varieties,
  78–79
'French Lace,' 83

G
Garden plans
  rose-clad arbor and
    walkway, 86–87
  roses and perennials,
    84–85
  rosy hillside, 88–89
'Gertrude Jekyll', 77, 89
'Gold Medal', 39
'Gourmet Popcorn', 51
Graft union, 10
'Graham Thomas', 59
Grandifloras, 36–39
  basic information, 36
  for bouquets, cutting,
    37
  for bouquets,
    selecting, 80
  cultivars, 38–39
Granular fertilizers, 14,
  15
Grape Hyacinth, 91
Griffith Buck roses, 56

< **92** >

H
'Hansa', 65
'Happy Trails', 48
Hardiness Zone, 6
'Harrison's Yellow', 66
Hedges
    best roses for, 74–75
    floribunda, 41, 74
    rejuvenating, 75
    shrub rose, 74
'Henry Hudson', 79
'Henry Kelsey', 55
'Heritage', 59, 89
'Hero', 89
Hillside garden plan,
    88–89
'Hi Neighbor', 39
Hips, ripening, 22
'Honey Perfume', 43
Hoses, soaker, 12
'Hot Cocoa', 43
'Hot Tamale', 83
Hybrid anemone, 91
Hybrid tea roses, 32–35
    basic information, 32
    for bouquets, 80
    containers for, 82
    cultivars, 34–35
    pruning, 33
Hydrangea, 87

I
'Iceberg', 43, 79, 89
'Ice Meidiland', 71
'Ingrid Bergman', 35, 83
Insecticidal soap, 30
Insects, 28–30
Integrated Pest
    Management (IPM),
    24–25
'Intrigue', 77
Iris, 91
Irrigation system, drip,
    12

J
Japanese beetles, 29

K
'Kardinal', 81
'Katherine Morley', 89
'Knock Out', 59, 75, 83
'Königin von Dänemark',
    67

L
Lady's Mantle, 85, 91
Lamb's-ears, 85, 91

Landscaping, 70–83. See
    also Garden plans
    arbors and
        pergolas, 72–73
    container-grown roses,
        82–83
    cutting flowers, 80–81
    fragrant flowers,
        78–79
    hedges, 74–75
    mixed borders, 76–77
    selecting roses for, 6
    shady conditions,
        70–71
Larkspur, 91
Lavender, 85, 91
'Lavender Cream', 76
Leafhoppers, 29
Liquid fertilizers, 14, 15
Lobelia, 89
'Love and Peace', 35, 81

M
'Margaret Merril', 89
'Margo Koster', 44
'Marie Pavié', 47
'Martha's Vineyard', 60
'May Night" Salvia, 91
Meidiland roses, 56
'Memorial Day', 35
Miniature roses, 48–51
    basic information, 48
    containers for, 82
    cultivars, 50–51
    feeding and pruning,
        49
    in garden plan, 85
    mulching, 49
    planting, 49
Minifloras, 48
'Minnie Pearl', 83
Miracle-Gro products
    Garden Soil, 9
    Garden Soil for Roses,
        9
    Shake 'n' Feed
    Continuous Release
        Rose Plant Food,
        14, 49
    Water Soluble Rose
        Plant Food, 14, 49
Mixed borders, 76–77
'Mme. Hardy', 67
'Morden Centennial', 61
'Mother's Day', 44
Mulch, 13, 21, 22
'Mutabilis', 68

N
Natural predators, 28
'Nearly Wild', 61, 75
'New Dawn', 55
New England aster, 91
Nicotiana, 89

O
Old garden and species
    roses, 62–68
    basic information,
        62
    for bouquets, 80–81
    cultivars, 64–68
    fragrance of, 78
    overgrown,
        rejuvenating, 63
    pruning, 63
    removing oldest
        canes, 63
Ornamental onion, 91
Ortho Bug-B-Gon
    products
        Garden &
            Landscape Insect
            Killer, 29, 30
        Japanese Beetle
            Killer, 29
        MAX Insect Killer
            for Lawns, 29
        Multi-Purpose
            Insect Killer
            Concentrate,
            28
        Multi-Purpose
            Insect Killer
            Ready-Spray,
            28
        Multi-Purpose
            Insect Killer
            Ready-to-Use,
            30
Ortho disease-control
    products
        Garden Disease
            Control, 26, 27
        Orthenex Insect &
            Disease Control,
            26, 27
        Systemic Insect
            Killer, 28, 29, 30
        Volck Oil Spray, 30
Ortho's Home Gardener's
    Problem
    Solver, 25

< 93 >

P
Pansy, 91
'Party Girl', 83
'Pat Austin', 77
Peony, 91
Perennials, 45, 76, 84–85
Pergolas, 72–73
Pests
    common types, 28–30
    controlling, 21, 24–25
    identifying, 25
    natural deterrents, 90
    natural predators for,
        28
'Peter Mayle', 77
Phlox, 89
Pinching flowers, 21
Pincushion flower, 89
Planting
    bare-root roses, 10–11
    container-grown roses,
        11
    preparing soil for, 8–9
    site selection, 8, 24
    spacing between
        plants, 9, 24
Plants, companion,
    90–91
Polyanthas, 44–47
    basic information, 44
    cultivars, 46–47
    growing with
        perennials, 45
    pruning, 45
Potted roses, 82
Powdery mildew, 26–27
'The Prince', 71
Pruning
    benefits of, 16
    fall and winter, 23
    gloves for, 16
    schedule for, 16
    spring, 18
    summer, 21
    techniques for, 16–17
    tools for, 17

Q
'Queen Elizabeth', 36
'Queen of Denmark', 67

R
'Rainbow's End', 51
Romantica roses, 84, 85
Rosa gallica officinalis,
    62, 64
'Rosa Mundi', 67
Rosa rugosa, 65
Rose aphids, 30, 90

Rosemary, 89
'Royal Highness', 81
Rust, 27

S
Sage, 85
'Sally Holmes', 61
Scale, 30
Scotts products
    Nature Scapes Color-
        Enhanced Mulch,
        13
    Rose & Bloom Slow
        Release Plant Food,
        14
Selection guide
    bare-root roses, 6–7
    container-grown roses,
        6
    hardiness zones, 6
    landscaping
        considerations, 6
    ordering new roses,
        23
    pest-resistant varieties,
        24
'Sevillana', 56
'Sexy Rexy', 81
Shady conditions, 8,
    70–71
'Sheer Bliss', 89
'Sheila's Perfume', 79
'Showbiz', 81
Shrub roses, 56–61
    basic information, 56
    containers for, 82
    cultivars, 58–61
    fertilizing, 57
    for hedges, 74
    mulching, 57
    pruning, 57
    watering, 57
Snowdrop, 91
Soaker hoses, 12
Soil, 8–9
'Sombreuil', 73, 81
Species roses. See Old
    garden and species
    roses
Spring care, 18–19
Spring companion
    plants, 91
'Starry Night', 75
Stonecrop, 85, 91
Summer care, 21
Summer companion
    plants, 91
'Sun Flare', 76
Sunlight, 8, 24

'Sun Sprinkles', 51
Sweet alyssum, 89

T
'The Fairy', 47
Thrips, 28
Transplanting roses, 19
Tree roses, 22
'Trumpeter', 76
Tulip, 91

U
Union, graft, 10

V
Verbena, 87, 91
Viola, 89
Vitamin B-1 solution, 10

W
Watering
    best methods, 12, 13
    best time of day, 13
    lack of, 12
    mulch and, 13
    newly-planted roses,
        11
    schedule for, 12, 13,
        25
    summer months, 21
    too much, 12
Water-soluble fertilizers,
    14, 15
Winter protection, 18,
    22–23
Wormwood, 91

Z
'Zéphirine Drouhin', 73

USDA HARDINESS ZONE MAP

This map of climate zones helps you select plants for your garden that will survive a typical winter in your region. The United States Department of Agriculture (USDA) developed the map, basing the zones on the lowest recorded temperatures across North America. Zone 1 is the coldest area and Zone 11 is the warmest.

Plants are classified by the coldest temperature and zone they can endure. For example, plants hardy to Zone 6 survive where winter temperatures drop to −10°F. Those hardy to Zone 8 die long before it's that cold. These plants may grow in colder regions but must be replaced each year. Plants rated for a range of hardiness zones can usually survive winter in the coldest region as well as tolerate the summer heat of the warmest one.

To find your hardiness zone, note the approximate location of your community on the map, then match the color band marking that area to the key.

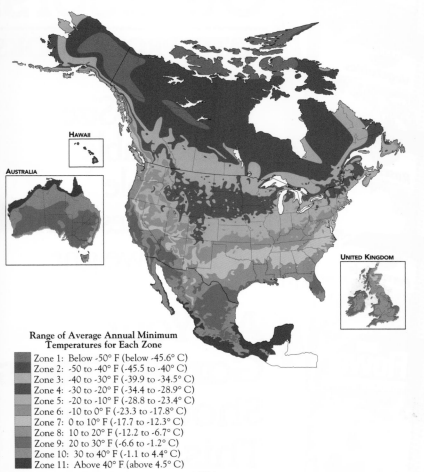

Range of Average Annual Minimum Temperatures for Each Zone

Zone 1: Below -50° F (below -45.6° C)
Zone 2: -50 to -40° F (-45.5 to -40° C)
Zone 3: -40 to -30° F (-39.9 to -34.5° C)
Zone 4: -30 to -20° F (-34.4 to -28.9° C)
Zone 5: -20 to -10° F (-28.8 to -23.4° C)
Zone 6: -10 to 0° F (-23.3 to -17.8° C)
Zone 7: 0 to 10° F (-17.7 to -12.3° C)
Zone 8: 10 to 20° F (-12.2 to -6.7° C)
Zone 9: 20 to 30° F (-6.6 to -1.2° C)
Zone 10: 30 to 40° F (-1.1 to 4.4° C)
Zone 11: Above 40° F (above 4.5° C)

< 95 >